Optimal Well-Being for Senior Adults II

Reproducible Activity Handouts Promoting Healthy Life Skills

Ester R.A. Leutenberg
Kathy A. Khalsa, CPC, OTR/L

Illustrated by
Amy L. Brodsky, LISW-S

Mandala Art by
Esther Piszczek, CZT

publisher of therapy, counseling, and self-help resources

101 West 2nd Street, Suite 203
Duluth, MN 55802

800-247-6789

Books@WholePerson.com
WholePerson.com

Optimal Well-Being for Senior Adults II
Reproducible Activity Handouts Promoting Healthy Life Skills

Copyright ©2017 by Ester R.A. Leutenberg and Kathy A. Khalsa. All rights reserved. The activities, assessment tools, and handouts in this workbook are reproducible by the purchaser for educational or therapeutic purposes. No other part of this book may be reproduced or transmitted in any form by any means, electronic or mechanical without permission in writing from the publisher.

All efforts have been made to ensure accuracy of the information contained in this workbook as of the date published. The author(s) and the publisher expressly disclaim responsibility for any adverse effects arising from the use or application of the information contained herein.

Printed in the United States of America

Editorial Director: Carlene Sippola
Art Director: Mathew Pawlak
Mandala Design: Esther Piszczek, CZT
Illustrator: Amy L. Brodsky, LISW-S

Library of Congress Control Number: 2016960488
ISBN:978-157025-351-5

INTRODUCTION

Optimal Well-Being for Senior Adults II
Introduction

Optimal Well-Being for Senior Adults II is the second in a series of workbooks consisting of reproducible activity handouts that will meet the needs of facilitators and their clients. The activities in the workbook are clear, easy-to-follow handouts written for mental health professionals to provide guidance and content to their senior clients.

It is written with the intent to be adapted, if needed, and then reproduced for an individual or a group. The handouts can be individualized to meet the specific needs of the participants. Creativity is encouraged by both the leader and participants in an ongoing process to generate satisfying and meaningful sessions.

The use of artwork, graphics, and different fonts offers interest and variety to enhance focus and attention to the topic at hand.

To aid the facilitator, each handout has a Leader's Guide written for the facilitator.
It includes the following:
- **Purpose** (identify the skill the participant will be learning)
- **Possible Names of Sessions** (offers three possible names for the session)
- **Background Information** (introduces the session)
- **Activity** (provides a step-by-step outline for how to lead the session)
- **Variations** (describes at least one variation different from the outlined activity)

Each of the ten chapters has five handouts with three levels of understanding.
This format encourages the facilitator to choose which level is most appropriate for the specific individuals to be served and avoid frustration of both the facilitator and group members.

Within each chapter the five handouts include the following:
- One handout: For Basic Level of understanding which is presented with more concrete concepts and simpler language.
- Three handouts: For an Intermediate Level of understanding for individuals who can easily sustain concentration and focus.
- One handout: For a High Level of understanding to be used with individuals with a full ability for listening, sharing, and developing insight.

The level of understanding icons will be on the cover page of each chapter and on the back of the activity handouts entitled The Leader's Guide.

The activity handouts for the participants are all …
- Activity-based allowing for client involvement
- Designed for specific, well-defined purposes
- Organized logically
- Reproducible
- User-friendly
- Visually appealing

The certificate on page 131 may be photocopied, filled in, and awarded to participants when they have completed their handouts.

**Although this workbook is intended for senior adults,
often referring to the 50+ age group, others may benefit from it as well.**

10 Valuable Tips for Facilitating Senior Adult Groups

Some helpful tips to consider when leading groups with seniors to ensure effective outcomes and to preemptively manage your possible frustration level:

1. At the beginning of the group session, establish if everyone can hear properly by asking, "Can everyone hear me?" If people answer "no," consider rearranging the seating to allow those who cannot hear to sit in another place, or you as the group leader, can change seats. If the people who sit across from you have seats with their backs to the wall, they might find that this improves their ability to hear.

2. Have an assortment of different pens and pencils to accommodate fine-motor coordination. Black pens will be easiest to read, especially with people who have visual impairments.

3. If the group room does not have tables, have magazines or clipboards handy to provide sturdy writing surfaces.

4. For organizational purposes, photocopy and then three-hole punch the handouts. Distribute three-hole folders or notebooks, or have pocket folders available for each participant.

5. To save time, file prepared handouts by levels in three separate notebooks:
    - One notebook for Basic Level handouts (10 handouts)
    - One notebook for Intermediate Level handouts (30 handouts)
    - One notebook for High Level handouts (10 handouts)

   This will allow you to quickly and easily find the appropriate handouts. You may also divide topics within the notebooks to offer the most appropriate handout for a specific group or individual.

6. Be aware of bathroom needs and accommodate the times of your groups accordingly.

7. If the ambient noise around the group interferes, make a sign saying "SHHHH … Group in Progress" to cue staff to lower their voices. Place the sign where the people passing by can easily see it.

8. If you determine during the group session that the handout and activity you chose was too difficult, or too easy, quickly adapt it rather than continuing. Find an easier or more challenging way to present the content of the handout, or have an alternate plan already photocopied and ready to go to avoid frustration for everyone (including you as the facilitator).

9. Feel free to elaborate on any topic provided. For example, when you present the topic of humor, tell group about something you have recently read or experienced. For instance: *"I recently read an article that pointed out that laughter can be the best medicine … it's good for your heart, immune system, brain health, and it increases pain tolerance."*

10. At the end of the session, ask group members what they learned or relearned from the session. In addition to gaining valuable feedback, it is useful for documentation purposes.

INTRODUCTION

Table of Contents – Sorted by Topics

Topic I – Anger 9
- My Anger Expression 11
- Understanding My Anger 13
- Anger Management: Acknowledge What It Is! 15
- My Anger Temperature 17
- Forgiveness … Giving Up the Anger 19

Topic II – Communication 21
- Communications with My Healthcare Provider 23
- What You Don't Say Counts Too 25
- Communications Interview 27
- Communication Works for People Who Work at It 29
- Tough Conversations 31

Topic III – Coping Skills 33
- Meds and Me 35
- A Self-Care Tool: H.A.L.T. 37
- Stressors, Coping Skills, & Supports 39
- Recipe for Disaster – Recipe for Survival 41
- Coping Skills Journal 43

Topic IV – Mental/Cognitive Disorders 45
- Stigma of Mental Illness 47
- Move Away from the Myths:
  - Anxiety 49
  - BiPolar Disorder 51
  - Depression 53
  - Dementia 55

Topic V – Positive Attitude 57
- What Makes You Joyous and Satisfied? 59
- Cultivating Gratitude 61
- Slow and Steady Wins the Race 63
- Same Old, Same Old? Not for Long! 65
- A Love Letter to Me 67

Topic VI – Relationships 69
- How to Make a Friend 71
- Healthy Relationships Word Search 73
- Developing Meaningful Relationships 75
- Seven Dating Guidelines 77
- Learn about Elder Abuse and Neglect 79

Topic VII – Resiliency 81
- What Does Being Resilient Look Like? 83
- Resiliency:
  - Enjoy, Explore, & Experiment 85
  - Imagine, Innovate, & Invent 87
  - Take It to the Limit 89
  - Involve Self in the Greater Good 91

Topic VIII – Safety 93
- Emergency Information 95
- Safety First 97
- Kitchen Safety 99
- Safe & Sound 101
- Fact Sheet 103

Topic IX – Mindfulness 105
- Mindfulness vs. Busy Mind 107
- Exploring My Journey 109
- Spiritual Themes 111
- Weathering Spiritual Seasons 113
- Mindful Practices 115

Topic X – Thinking Skills 117
- Steps to a Healthy Brain 119
- Crossword Puzzle 121
- Keep on Thinking 123
- Stretch Your Mind 125
- Haiku Fun 127

Bonus 129
- Certificate of Completion 131
- My Mandala 133

Table of Contents
Activity Handouts Sorted in Alphabetical Order

Activity Handout	Topic	Page
A Love Letter to Me	Positive Attitude	67
A Self-Care Tool: H.A.L.T.	Coping Skills	37
Anger Management: Acknowledge What It Is!	Anger	15
Certificate of Completion	Bonus	131
Communication Works for People Who Work at It	Communication	29
Communications Interview	Communication	27
Communications with My Healthcare Provider	Communication	23
Coping Skills Journal	Coping Skills	43
Crossword Puzzle	Thinking Skills	121
Cultivating Gratitude	Positive Attitude	61
Developing Meaningful Relationships	Relationships	75
Emergency Information	Safety	95
Exploring My Journey	Mindfulness	109
Fact Sheet	Safety	103
Forgiveness … Giving Up the Anger	Anger	19
Haiku Fun	Thinking Skills	127
Healthy Relationships Word Search	Relationships	73
How to Make a Friend	Relationships	71
Keep on Thinking	Thinking Skills	123
Kitchen Safety	Safety	99
Learn about Elder Abuse and Neglect	Relationships	79
Meds and Me	Coping Skills	35
Mindful Practices	Mindfulness	115
Mindfulness vs. Busy Mind	Mindfulness	107
Move Away from the Myths: Anxiety	Mental and Cognitive Disorders	49
Move Away from the Myths: Bipolar Disorder	Mental and Cognitive Disorders	51
Move Away from the Myths: Dementia	Mental and Cognitive Disorders	53
Move Away from the Myths: Depression	Mental and Cognitive Disorders	55
My Anger Expression	Anger	11
My Anger Temperature	Anger	17
My Mandala	Bonus	133
Recipe for Disaster – Recipe for Survival	Coping Skills	41
Resiliency: Enjoy, Explore, & Experiment	Resiliency	85
Resiliency: Imagine, Innovate, & Invent	Resiliency	87
Resiliency: Involve Self in the Greater Good	Resiliency	91
Resiliency: Take It to the Limit	Resiliency	89
Safe & Sound	Safety	101
Safety First	Safety	97
Same Old, Same Old? Not for Long!	Positive Attitude	65
Seven Dating Guidelines	Relationships	77
Slow and Steady Wins the Race	Positive Attitude	63
Spiritual Themes	Mindfulness	111
Steps to a Healthy Brain	Thinking Skills	119
Stigma of Mental Illness	Mental and Cognitive Disorders	47
Stressors, Coping Skills, & Supports	Coping Skills	39
Stretch Your Mind	Thinking Skills	125
Understanding My Anger	Anger	13
Tough Conversations	Communication	31
Weathering Spiritual Seasons	Mindfulness	113
What Does Being Resilient Look Like?	Resiliency	83
What Makes You Joyous and Satisfied?	Positive Attitude	59
What You Don't Say Counts Too	Communication	25

INTRODUCTION

*We dedicate this workbook to the senior adults
who have inspired us in the past, who inspire us today,
and to those who will continue to inspire us in the future.*

Ester Leutenberg   *Kathy Khalsa*

Our thanks to the following professionals who make us look good!

Art Director – Mathew Pawlak
Editorial Director – Carlene Sippola
Illustrator – Amy L. Brodsky, LISW-S
Mandala Art – Esther Piszczek, CZT
Editor and Lifelong Teacher – Eileen Regen, MEd, CJE
Proofreader – Jay Leutenberg, CASA
Reviewer – Carol Butler, MS Ed, RN, C
Contributor – Kris Lowden, MA

Thanks to
The Guidance Group

and to the
Meaningful Life Skills Contributors

Rebecca J. August, LCSW
Vicki L. Addison, COTA
Melissa L. Oliver, OTR/L, MS
Judith A. Lutz, BA
Linda Prib, ADC
Joann Rascati
Sue Ellen Rosenblum, MOT, OTR/L
Libby D. Schardt, OTR/L
Donald Shields, BRE, MTS
Shelly Lynn Young, MSW

Topic 1

ANGER

Table of Contents and Corresponding Goals for Each Section

> Holding on to anger is like grasping a hot coal with the intent of throwing it at someone else; you are the one who gets burned.
> ~ Buddha

My ANGER Expression 11
To promote healthy anger expression with a simple format: I feel angry when …

Understanding My Anger 13
To develop awareness of how we manage our anger, including what provokes anger and how families of origin have influenced our anger management.

Anger Management: ACKNOWLEDGE WHAT IS! 15
To learn ways to manage anger effectively.

My Anger TEMPERATURE 17
To explore causes of anger and ways to cope with anger.

Forgiveness … Giving Up the Anger 19
To approach forgiveness as a way to release grudges and resolve past hurts.

LEVEL OF UNDERSTANDING

 Basic Level    Intermediate Level    High Level

My ANGER Expression

I feel anger when ...

Holding anger IN can be harmful to you!
         **Allowing uncontrolled anger OUT can
                           be harmful to you and others!**

**We don't become angry only when we are senior adults.
We have experienced anger since we were very young, even as babies and toddlers.
Have you ever seen a baby lose a rattle or a toddler have a toy taken out of his or her hands?**

The following format is useful for finding a way to express anger in a clear and effective way.
Complete any five of the statements below.

1. I feel angry when I hear the news that _____
   _____

2. I feel angry when my daughter is in _____
   _____

3. I feel angry when my sister or brother _____
   _____

4. I feel angry when my doctor or nurse _____
   _____

5. I feel angry when another driver _____
   _____

6. I feel angry when my neighbor _____
   _____

7. I feel angry when my partner _____
   _____

8. I feel angry when the government _____
   _____

9. I feel angry when I can't _____
   _____

10. I feel angry when I call somewhere for information and _____
    _____

My ANGER Expression
Leader's Guide

PURPOSE
To promote healthy anger expression with a simple format: "I feel angry when …"

POSSIBLE NAMES OF SESSIONS
- *Meet Your Anger*
- *I Feel Angry When*
- *ANGER – it's not new!*

BACKGROUND INFORMATION
Senior adults may have a lot to be angry about. They have lived with years of possible losses, disappointments, and betrayals. They may have held onto their anger for many years. Using prompts, they may be able to learn new and healthy ways to express anger.

ACTIVITY
1. Explain purpose and background to group using Background Information.
2. Distribute handouts and pens.
3. Allow group members ten minutes to complete the handouts.
4. Divide groups into pairs for sharing.
5. Reconvene and ask if participants had any commonalities with his/her partner. Share responses.
6. Discuss that healthy anger expression may improve life in many ways:
   a. relationships
   b. sleep
   c. blood pressure
   d. medication reductions
   e. overall well-being

VARIATIONS
1) Have all group members sit in a circle with a parachute and a small ball in the center. Go around the circle asking what people are angry about. They can give responses one-by-one when they pop the ball into the air with that last burst of energy with the parachute.
2) On the board or flip chart, list group members' ideas for completing the prompt, "I feel angry when …" Consider using these for future group sessions.

NOTES
_____
_____
_____
_____
_____
_____
_____
_____
_____
_____

Topic 1 — ANGER

Understanding My Anger

**Many of us would like to change the way we manage our anger.
Before we can establish new patterns for handling anger in our own lives,
we need to understand the old patterns that influenced us
and the implications of our anger management.**

1. When my mother (grandmother or female primary caregiver) became angry, she _____
   _____

2. When my father (grandfather or male primary caregiver) became angry, he _____
   _____

3. As a child, when I became angry, I _____
   _____

4. As a child, I learned … *(choose the one that is closest to the truth.)*

   ☐ It is okay to talk about my anger.

   ☐ Anger is scary.

   ☐ It is better to be happy. Don't be angry.

   ☐ Other _____

5. The people I am closest to say that my anger is _____
   _____

6. The worst aspect about my anger is:

   ☐ It is self-destructive   ☐ It impacts my relationships   ☐ Other _____
   _____

7. Who would appreciate your efforts in anger management?

   ☐ partner   ☐ primary doctor   ☐ friend   ☐ relative   ☐ co-workers   ☐ neighbor

   ☐ other _____

OPTIMAL WELL-BEING FOR SENIOR ADULTS II

Understanding My Anger
Leader's Guide

PURPOSE
To develop awareness of how we manage our anger, including what provokes anger and how families of origin have influenced our anger management.

POSSIBLE NAMES OF SESSIONS
- *I Have Choices About My Anger*
- *Out with the Old, In with the New*
- *Looking at the 'Other' Side*

BACKGROUND INFORMATION
The way we handle our anger has been strongly influenced by those who raised us. We may not have had positive role-models for handling this powerful emotion. We look at the ways our parents or caregivers dealt with anger, not to blame them, but to better understand our own behavior. In order to establish new patterns in our own lives, we need to understand the old patterns that may continue to shape us.

ACTIVITY
1. Distribute handouts and pens.
2. Encourage participants to complete the sentences with the first thoughts that come to mind. Emphasize that there are no right or wrong answers.
3. Discuss the responses as a group. If your group is large, you may wish to break into smaller groups. Groups of four work best.
4. Encourage participants to share their responses to the questions, but do not force them to do so.
5. Use the discussion to make several points:
    a. Our parents (or those who raised us) play a powerful role in shaping the way we handle anger. Sometimes we have modeled ourselves on one of our parents or caregivers, even if we didn't intend to. Sometimes we have selected a way of dealing with anger that is opposite of our parents or caregivers.
    b. Although our childhood experiences may have influenced the way we deal with anger, they do not need to determine how we deal with our anger presently.
    c. Most of us have more than one way of dealing with anger. We can learn to build on the positive responses and decrease the negative ones. Emphasize that change is possible.
6. Process with group members: discuss insights gained and possible changes in anger management styles.
7. Develop a list of responses to the question: What is one positive way I, or those I have observed, deal with anger? As participants identify particular strategies that have worked for them, ask them to share specific situations in which they have used those strategies successfully.

VARIATIONS
Develop a master list from responses to question number 7 from the *Understanding My Anger* handout. Create goals based on a discussion of these with plans for follow up.

NOTES
_____
_____
_____
_____
_____

Topic I — ANGER

Anger Management: ACKNOWLEDGE WHAT IS!

Anger is an emotion. It is a normal human response. When anger becomes too intense, when it happens too quickly and too often, and when it harms self and others, it is time to face it because anger can become destructive. Hostility may result in aggressive behavior. **Acknowledge the following four steps.**

1. "I'm angry"
This awareness is the first step in anger management. This anger may result from a feeling of being threatened, or from not having power, control, or independence. It may stem from feelings of lacking freedom or that "I don't belong."

2. Certain choices are not OK
- Acting harmfully or violently towards myself
- Acting harmfully or violently towards others

3. Anger not handled properly can result in …
Aggressive behavior   Guilty feelings
Depression   Health consequences
Elder abuse   Isolation

4. Healthy choices you have and can make!

When I am in situations where I find myself becoming angry, I have choices:

Leave the situation.

"I can leave a situation by _____."

Journal with a prompt.

"I feel/felt angry when _____."

Talk about it.

"I will talk about it to _____."

Other

_____

_____

Anger Management: ACKNOWLEDGE WHAT IS!
Leader's Guide

PURPOSE
To manage anger effectively.

POSSIBLE NAMES OF SESSIONS
- *If I Don't Learn to Manage My Anger, Then …*
- *Anger*
- *Sometimes, I See Red*

BACKGROUND INFORMATION
Anger, in and of itself, is not bad. It can make you feel alive and move you to getting something done. But, if anger is not handled well it can be destructive and unhealthy. It is important to emphasize choices.

ACTIVITY
1. Offer a few examples of stories you have recently heard that resulted in someone being angry.
2. Ask others to share the same.
3. Explain that very rarely do people like the feeling of anger or talking about this topic.
4. Distribute handouts and pens.
5. Review aloud Steps 1, 2, and 3 with focus on step 3, acknowledging the negative results of not handling anger well.
6. Complete Step 4 together as a group sharing responses.
7. Close the group asking each participant to complete this sentence:
   If I don't learn to manage my anger, then _____.

VARIATIONS
1) Discuss medical problems that might be related to anger issues.
2) Lead a guided imagery exercise about anger and forgiveness.

NOTES

Topic I — ANGER

My Anger TEMPERATURE

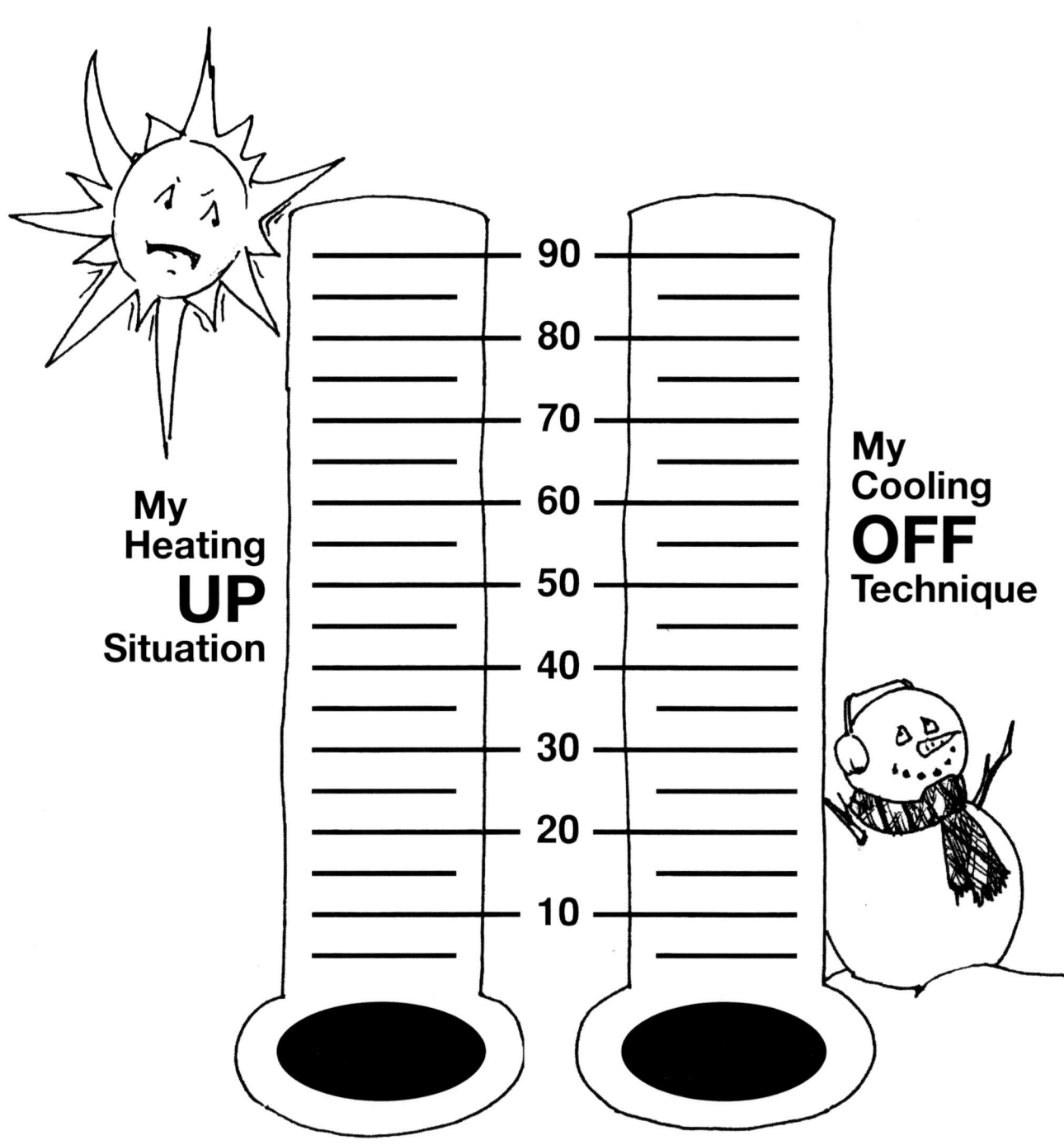

OPTIMAL WELL-BEING FOR SENIOR ADULTS II

My Anger TEMPERATURE
Leader's Guide

PURPOSE
To explore causes of anger and ways to cope with anger.

POSSIBLE NAMES OF SESSIONS
- *What Fuels My Anger?*
- *Hot and Cold*
- *Chill Out*

BACKGROUND INFORMATION
Everyone gets angry from time to time. It is natural to have those feelings. What is important is the reaction to these feelings and how one copes with anger. It is also important to be able to recognize what triggers anger. Repeated anger reactions are harmful to the body, mind, and spirit.

ACTIVITY
1. Introduce the topic of anger. Distribute color pens or pencils.
2. Review Background Information.
3. Introduce the idea of the body being like a thermometer. Explain that as we become angry, our temperatures rise. This could be harmful to our bodies as well as our relationships. Coping skills or calming strategies are needed to cool off.
4. Copy a thermometer on the board. Use this scale: **10-30 – minimal anger – warm; 30-60 – moderate anger – getting hot; 60-90 – severe anger – on fire**
5. Ask group members to listen as situations are read that may or may not result in anger. As each situation is read, ask group members to use the scale on the board to judge their possible reaction. Then ask them to color the corresponding number of degrees in the thermometer labeled "Heating UP."
6. Relate situations that might elicit anger. Examples: You are left out of a family get-together." After you already said you couldn't, you are asked again to take care of the grandchildren for a weekend. "You overhear someone in the grocery store making fun of a person who is older and can't hear well." Use actual examples from the group to make this relevant.
7. After reading each situation, ask volunteers to shade in the thermometer on the board to see how hot they are (where they stopped coloring). This temperature is to be marked on the second thermometer on the board, labeled "Cooling OFF."
8. Write this new scale on the board. **-0 – Does not cool me off; -5 – Chilly; -10 – Frozen**
9. Read a series of coping skills and calming strategies to the group. As each strategy is read, ask group members to use a new scale on the board to determine how well this strategy would work. For example, a strategy that really helps would decrease the temperature by 10 degrees and a strategy that doesn't help would not decrease the temperature at all. Group members are to begin at the temperature marked from the "Heating UP" exercise and color corresponding numbers of degrees down. Examples of coping skills and calming strategies: Take slow, deep breaths, go for a walk, talk to a friend, work out, seek professional help.
10. After several strategies as suggested, distribute the handouts and markers.
11. Ask group members to complete the handout and discuss their insights.

VARIATIONS
1) Before the session begins, or in a separate meeting, ask group members to write on index cards some examples of anger-provoking, real life situations. Use these cards for anger prompts for that group.
2) Before the group session begins, or in a separate meeting, ask group members to write on index cards some calming strategies or coping skills. Use these cards as prompts for the group.

Topic 1 — ANGER

Forgiveness ... Giving Up the Anger

Forgiveness may be one of the most difficult tasks we do as humans. It may seem impossible to forgive at times or it might not be what we want to do, but it may be a wise choice.

The possible impact of NOT forgiving:

- Anger
- Health issues
- Impaired relationships

- _____
- _____
- _____

In general, how do you see yourself ... as a forgiving or an unforgiving person?
(put an X on the continuum line below)

UNFORGIVING 0 _____ 10 FORGIVING

What is one forgiveness issue you have in your life right now? _____
_____

Where are you on the continuum line on the above forgiveness issue?

UNFORGIVING 0 _____ 10 FORGIVING

People who have forgiven (or reconciled) have reported feeling "not conquered by bitterness" and "not giving the person who hurt them the power."

How might you feel if you move more to the forgiving side? _____
_____

If you had the opportunity to express your feelings to the above person, what would you say? _____
_____
_____

What steps can you take to give yourself the gift of forgiving another?

1. _____
2. _____
3. _____

Forgiveness ... Giving Up the Anger
Leader's Guide

PURPOSE
To approach forgiveness as a way to release and resolve past hurts.

POSSIBLE NAMES OF SESSIONS
- *Forgive and Forget?*
- *Steps to Forgiveness*
- *Am I Forgiving?*

BACKGROUND INFORMATION
Forgiveness is an often overlooked topic by the healthcare system and left to theologians. Unfortunately, forgiveness issues may slip through the cracks and be left unresolved or not discussed. In turn, this may be damaging to a person's well-being.

ACTIVITY
1. Discuss that forgiving and forgetting an issue with another person is not actually possible. We might forgive, but we do not forget. *(Will the mother who forgives the drunk driver who hit her daughter ever forget?)* One advantage of remembering is that it teaches us life lessons and reminds us of how we want to act and how we expect others to act as well.
2. Distribute handouts and pens.
3. Give group members fifteen minutes to complete the handout. Emphasize that not forgiving is not an option. Use therapeutic judgement if a participant expresses difficulty in forgiving.
4. Share responses in an attitude of acceptance.
5. Discuss what the next step might be in the healing process for each group member.

VARIATIONS
1) Raise thought-provoking questions around the topic of forgiveness:
   a. Is it ever all right NOT to forgive?
   b. What are the reasons that people do not forgive?
   c. What are the benefits of forgiving?
2) Encourage participants to explore early messages about forgiveness:
   a. Did you live with forgivers or grudge-bearers when you were growing up?
   b. Did you ever know any grudge-bearers who couldn't even remember what they were angry about?
3) Explore these quotes about forgiveness:
   a. *The weak can never forgive. Forgiveness is the attribute of the strong.*
      ~ Mahatma Gandhi
   b. *Forgive others not because they deserve forgiveness, but because you deserve peace.*
      ~ Jonathan Lockwood Hule
   c. *It's one of the greatest gifts you can give to yourself, to forgive. Forgive everybody.*
      ~ Maya Angelou

NOTES
_____
_____
_____
_____

Topic II

COMMUNICATION

Table of Contents and Corresponding Goals for Each Section

> *I'm a great believer that any tool that enhances communication has profound effects in terms of how people can learn from each other, and how they can achieve the kind of freedoms that they're interested in.*
>
> ~ Bill Gates

Communications with My Healthcare Provider 23
To provide a tool for healthcare recipients to give to healthcare providers to ensure thorough communications.

What You DON'T Say Counts Too 25
To demonstrate the impact of nonverbal communication.

Communication Interview 27
To identify personal ways of communicating to gain positive communication experiences.

Communication Works For People Who Work At It 29
To self-evaluate both "good" and "bad" communication topics to promote effective communication.

Tough Conversations 31
To increase communication skills by getting practice in dealing with difficult or tough conversational topics.

LEVEL OF UNDERSTANDING

Basic Level | Intermediate Level | High Level

Topic II — COMMUNICATION

Communication with My Healthcare Provider

My healthcare provider's name _____

1. I took my meds ...
   ___ exactly as prescribed
   ___ more or less as you prescribed
   ___ not at all as you prescribed

2. My chief problem(s) is_____
   _____

   It affects me because_____
   _____

3. My questions:
   _____?
   _____?

Completed by _____ Date _____

My healthcare provider's name _____

1. I took my meds ...
   ___ exactly as prescribed
   ___ more or less as you prescribed
   ___ not at all as you prescribed

2. My chief problem(s) is_____
   _____

   It affects me because_____
   _____

3. My questions:
   _____?
   _____?

Completed by _____ Date _____

OPTIMAL WELL-BEING FOR SENIOR ADULTS II

Communication with My Healthcare Provider
Leader's Guide

PURPOSE
To provide a tool for healthcare recipients to give to healthcare providers to ensure thorough communications.

POSSIBLE NAMES OF SESSIONS
- *Follow Up Is Hard to Do*
- *Being Prepared for My Healthcare Provider*
- *I'm Ready Now!*

BACKGROUND INFORMATION
Oftentimes, when people go to their healthcare providers, they present less than a full picture of their current health status. Anxiety, disorganization, and forgetfulness account for a few obstacles to full disclosure.

ACTIVITY
1. This activity is meant to be in a group setting to practice.
2. Distribute handouts and pens.
3. Explain the purpose of the handout using background information for discussion.
4. Give group members five to ten minutes to complete the top half.
5. Role play meeting with healthcare provider using the handout as a guide.
6. Tell participants they can use the bottom half for their next visit to their healthcare provider.
7. Distribute one additional handout to group members for future photocopying.

VARIATIONS
Meet with family members. Distribute handouts and explain purpose: To support proper healthcare visits using this communications tool.

NOTES
_____
_____
_____
_____
_____
_____
_____
_____
_____
_____
_____
_____
_____
_____

What You DON'T Say Counts Too!

Impressions:

1. _____

2. _____

3. _____

OPTIMAL WELL-BEING FOR SENIOR ADULTS II

What You DON'T Say Counts Too!
Leader's Guide

PURPOSE
To demonstrate the impact of nonverbal communication.

POSSIBLE NAMES OF SESSIONS
- *Miss-Communications*
- *What Am I Not Saying?*
- *Perceptions or Misperceptions?*

BACKGROUND INFORMATION
As we age, we might lose leisure interests, spiritual supports, anger outlets, and social supports. People move or pass away. Physical limitations prevent leisure and anger outlets. It is possible to take action to ensure that these important survival skills are still intact.

ACTIVITY
1. Introduce the concept of nonverbal communication, either by people role-playing or by showing magazine clippings.
2. Distribute handouts and pens.
3. Ask group members to look at the three drawings on the handout and write their first assumption based on each person in the drawing.
4. Share responses.
5. Allow group members to provide other opinions about the people in the picture.
6. Develop questions one might ask to validate or negate any possible assumptions. This is the first question to answer: "How would we know if what we thought was true?"
7. Now, ask group members to consider that they might be viewed as the pictures on the page. Someone like a roommate, friend, family member, or healthcare professional might be assuming something about a person is doing or why the person is acting in a certain way. The assumption might be incorrect.

VARIATIONS
1) Write four words on individual slips of paper.
   - tired
   - angry
   - bothered
   - interested

   One by one, invite four people to pick a slip of paper and "act" in a non-verbal way in front of the room. Ask group members to write their impressions when they look at each person. Discuss perceptions and misperceptions.
2) Emphasize that trying to understand people by their nonverbal communication, and without conversation, can be a disaster. The likelihood of misunderstanding is great. Ask group members to write a short (even funny) skit taken from real-life examples, and to perform this in front of the group as a follow up session.

NOTES
_____
_____
_____
_____

Communication Interview

A. Interview a partner and circle and/or write the responses:

1. Is it easy or difficult for you to talk to people who you do not know?   **Easy   Difficult**

2. Do you prefer large social events or small get-togethers?
   Large social events   Small get togethers

3. Do you prefer talking about "small talk" or "deep issues"?
   Small talk   Deep Issues

4. How do you rate your ability to talk about your feelings? Use a scale of
   1 (not so great) to 10 (great)   1   2   3   4   5   6   7   8   9   10

5. Do you give too few details to people, just enough, or do you give too many details?
   Too few details   Just enough   Too many details

6. When you are upset, do you tend to cry, scream, or isolate yourself, or do you do something else?   **Cry   Scream   Isolate**

   Something else:_____

7. Fill in the blank: I know I shouldn't talk about_____
   _____but I do it anyways.

8. Which are you better at: **Clearly expressing yourself?   Being a good listener?**

9. Which one is more true of you:
   Thinking about your words carefully before you speak?   Thinking as you speak?

B. After the interview, thank your partner. Then write a few words of your impressions about how your partner communicates. Include anything you noticed (eye contact, voice volume, content, body, posture, etc.).

_____
_____
_____
_____
_____

C. Introduce your partner to the group and include the information from sections A and B.

_____

OPTIMAL WELL-BEING FOR SENIOR ADULTS II

Communication Interview
Leader's Guide

PURPOSE
To identify personal ways of communicating.

To gain communication experience.

POSSIBLE NAMES OF SESSIONS
- *How Do I Communicate?*
- *You're Being Interviewed!*
- *Let's Talk!*

BACKGROUND INFORMATION
This interview format asks questions about personal communications. Sometimes we can gain clarity and insight if someone asks the right questions at the right time. In addition, this activity provides multiple opportunities for positive communication experiences:
1) interviewing
2) being interviewed
3) observing another person as a communicator
4) introducing the partner in front of a group

ACTIVITY
1. Divide group into pairs. Include yourself if there is an odd number of participants.
2. Explain concept of the handout and distribute a pen and a handout to each individual.
3. Allow seven minutes per interview.
4. Ask individuals to introduce their partners.
5. Ask group members to identify one item they learned about themselves and one item they learned about the other person.

VARIATIONS
1) Ask group members if they would like additional handouts to use with friends and/or family members.
2) Suggest that group members, as a whole or in small teams, discuss a topic of general interest to practice talking and listening skills

NOTES
_____
_____
_____
_____
_____
_____
_____
_____
_____
_____
_____
_____
_____
_____
_____

Topic II — COMMUNICATION

Communication Works!

EXPLORE YOUR TOP GOOD AND BAD COMMUNICATION HABITS.

GOOD COMMUNICATION HABITS	BAD COMMUNICATION HABITS
☐ Making good eye contact	☐ Interrupting
☐ Asking clarifying questions	☐ Thinking about what you are going to say rather than listening
☐ Trying to understand the other's point of view	☐ Not asking questions
☐ Being brief and to the point	☐ Changing topics abruptly
☐ Using tact	☐ Using offensive nonverbal communication
☐ Remembering … it is okay to be silent	☐ Telling people what to do
☐ Using language that the listener can understand and relate to	☐ Making promises you cannot keep
☐ Using the person's name	☐ Name calling or blaming
☐ Listening to what is said … and not said	☐ Talking too loudly
☐ Staying focused	☐ Becoming distracted

Communication works for those who work at it.

~ John Powell

Communication Works!
Leader's Guide

PURPOSE

To self-evaluate both "good" and "bad" communication habits to promote effective communication.

POSSIBLE NAMES OF SESSIONS
- *Top 10 Lists*
- *HABITS: Good and Bad*
- *You Need to Work at It!*

BACKGROUND INFORMATION

Effective communication is a lifelong skill requiring ongoing work. Many senior adults find themselves in unexpected new social, and possibly work, roles. It may be timely to pause and think about both good and bad communication habits to establish healthy bonds in relationships.

ACTIVITY

1. Distribute handouts and pens.
2. Discuss each point on both sides offering examples as you go.
3. Brainstorm other "good" habits (example: smiling, using appropriate humor in conversation) and "bad" habits (example: not hearing well and pretending to hear).
4. Ask group members to check off their top "good" habits and "bad" habits.
5. Assist group members in developing realistic goals or action plans to increase "good" communication habits and decrease "bad" communication habits.

VARIATIONS

1) Discuss the quotation at the bottom of the handout.
2) Research pertinent communication quotations and share with the group.
3) Ask group members to look up inspirational quotations about communication and bring them in to discuss as a group.

NOTES

Topic II — COMMUNICATION

Tough Conversations

For most people, communicating with others is easily done with easy topics. However, conversations are more challenging and interesting with moderate and difficult topics. Below is a way of viewing the topics you talk about.

Easy Topics (Basic Skill)	Moderate Topics (Intermediate Skill)	Difficult Topics (Advanced Skill)
• **NEUTRAL ISSUES** Movies, books, music, weather, food, fashion, local events	• **MODERATE ISSUES** Current events if not too "hot," goals, travel experiences, future plans, job duties, responsibilities	• **DEEP ISSUES** Money, religion, politics, intense legal issues, sensitive or controversial topics
• **GOOD NEWS** Births, marriages, celebrations	• **MILD TO MODERATE NEWS THAT PRESENTS SOME DEGREE OF CONFLICT** Not getting a raise, children not visiting, candidate not getting elected.	• **BAD NEWS** Divorce, illness, death, unexpected change, awkward situations
• **SUPERFICIAL FEELINGS**	• **FEELINGS NOT SUPERFICIAL OR DEEP**	• **DEEP FEELINGS or CONFLICTED FEELINGS**
• **NOTES** _____ _____ _____ _____ _____ _____ _____ _____ _____	• **NOTES** _____ _____ _____ _____ _____ _____ _____ _____ _____	• **NOTES** _____ _____ _____ _____ _____ _____ _____ _____ _____

OPTIMAL WELL-BEING FOR SENIOR ADULTS II

Tough Conversations
Leader's Guide

PURPOSE

To reinforce communication skills by practicing how to deal with tough conversation topics.

POSSIBLE NAMES OF SESSIONS
- *Role Plays*
- *Learning How to Have Difficult Conversations*
- *Tough Can Be Interesting!*

BACKGROUND INFORMATION

Tough topics can be very stressful for many people to discuss. They are often accompanied by avoidance, apprehension, fear, and feelings of pending doom.

ACTIVITY

1. Present the concept that easy topics are associated with a basic skill, medium topics require an intermediate skill, and difficult or tough topics require an advanced skill.
2. Distribute handouts and pens.
3. Engage group members in a brief discussion of easy and medium topics. Encourage note-taking as needed.
4. Focus on the advanced skill of dealing with controversial or tough topics using group members' examples. Encourage note-taking.
5. Role play group generated examples or use the following examples:
   a. Tell your children and grandchildren that you do not have money for gifts.
   b. Tell your neighbors that their front yard is unsightly.
   c. Tell your spouse something for which you feel guilty.

   Coach role plays to include the following parameters:
   a. Preface the communication with a preliminary statement: I know this is a sensitive topic.
   b. Be brief and to the point.
   c. End the conversation by thanking the listener(s) for sharing time.
6. Process by asking what group members learned and encourage them to build confidence by practice.

VARIATIONS

Create a file of articles from local newspapers about potentially difficult/tough topics for further exploration.

NOTES

_____
_____
_____
_____
_____
_____
_____
_____
_____
_____

Topic III
COPING SKILLS
Table of Contents and Corresponding Goals for Each Section

Problems are not the problem; coping is the problem.
~ Virginia Satir

Meds and ME 35
To promote the coping skills of taking medications properly.

A Self-Care Tool: H.A.L.T. 37
To promote the coping skill of exploring four triggering emotions, learning to H.A.L.T. and explore ways to address these triggers.

Stressors, Coping Skills, & Supports 39
To assist with coping skills and supportive system development.

Recipe for Disaster – Recipe for Survival 41
To explore the coping skills (ingredients) of knowing what factors contribute to successes and disasters.

Coping Skills Journal 43
To reinforce coping skills by actively journaling and repeatedly asking the question, "How did you take care of yourself?"

LEVEL OF UNDERSTANDING

 Basic Level  Intermediate Level  High Level

Topic III — COPING SKILLS

Meds and ME

Medications can be an effective health treatment for senior adults, but only when taken safely.

Please check the statements that are true for you.

- ☐ I am able to open my medicine containers easily.
- ☐ I ask the pharmacist about side effects of a new prescription.
- ☐ I can read the directions on the labels of my medicine containers.
- ☐ I check to find foods or activities to avoid when I have a new prescription filled.
- ☐ I faithfully tell my healthcare provider(s) about past problems with prescriptions when other medicines are being considered.
- ☐ I follow the dosage schedule as closely as possible.
- ☐ I know the side effects of my medicines.
- ☐ I never take anyone else's medicines.
- ☐ I only take medications that are prescribed by my healthcare provider.
- ☐ I read the product information that comes with my prescriptions.
- ☐ I regularly discard old medicines.
- ☐ I report any problems I am having with medicines to my healthcare provider.
- ☐ I share my complete list of current medications with every one of my healthcare providers, so each one will know what the other one is prescribing.
- ☐ I use a pillbox to organize myself.
- ☐ My pharmacist and/or my healthcare provider(s) make sure that my medications are compatible.

_____ Total check marks

```
    15    ✔ = Excellent
  13 - 14 ✔ = Good
  11 - 12 ✔ = Fair
   9 - 10 ✔ = Need Improvement
    0 - 8 ✔ = UH-OH!
```

OPTIMAL WELL-BEING FOR SENIOR ADULTS II

MEDS and Me
Leader's Guide

PURPOSE
To promote the coping skill of taking medications properly.

POSSIBLE NAMES OF SESSIONS
- *Me and My Medications*
- *Taking My Meds Right*
- *My Body! My responsibility!*

BACKGROUND INFORMATION
Taking medications properly can be a challenge for senior adults. They may be at greater health risks because they may take several medications at one time. Chronic illnesses coupled with acute illnesses can be a complicated factor as well. Changes in the body may account for unexpected reactions from over the counter or prescribed medications. Another complication may be non-compatible medications taken simultaneously.

ACTIVITY
1. List the different medications and other substances people in the group use. They may include some or all of the following:
   - Herbal remedies
   - Over-the-counter medicines
   - Laxatives
   - Vitamins
   - Antacids
   - Alcohol
   - Prescribed medicines for physical or emotional symptoms
2. Explain that medicine-taking may be complicated.
3. Distribute handouts and pens.
4. Instruct group members to complete the handout.
5. Discuss each item, allowing different people to share.
6. Problem solve obstacles that might arise if boxes are not checked.
7. Review scores in box to see how group members ranked.

VARIATIONS
1) Divide group members into pairs.
2) Complete the handouts and allow for pairs to share and discuss which boxes are checked. Problem solve.
3) Bring a drug reference manual, internet site information, and other resources to expand participants' awareness of ways to find information about medicines.

NOTES
_____
_____
_____
_____
_____
_____
_____
_____
_____
_____

Topic III — COPING SKILLS

A Self-Care Tool: H.A.L.T.

The H.A.L.T. acronym comes from the addictions recovery process and stands for
Hungry – Angry – Lonely – Tired

Typically, when we experience any of these four feelings, we get into trouble! Undesirable behaviors are likely to happen: watching too much TV, worrying excessively, falling back into beliefs about ourselves that result in shame or guilt, alcohol or drugs, gambling, etc.

H

HUNGRY: hunger for food, hunger for attention, hunger for understanding, hunger for touch, hunger for appreciation, hunger for acceptance.

IDEA: community involvement _____
_____
_____
_____
_____

A

ANGRY: criticism of self and others, belittling self and others, engagement in physical violence and destructive behaviors.

IDEA: prayer for ourselves and others, physical activity for outlet, taking time out to breathe, search for underlying cause of anger, counseling, identity, making a request to gain back perceived or actual loss of power or control.
_____
_____
_____

L

LONELY: self isolation, difficulty in reaching out, difficulty in accepting help.

IDEA: community, counseling _____
_____
_____
_____
_____

T

TIRED: feeling overloaded, overwhelmed, physically or mentally tired.

IDEA: cut back on activities or commitments, take breathing breaks with fresh air if possible, vacation, nap, get quality sleep.
_____
_____
_____
_____

A Self-Care Tool: H.A.L.T.
Leader's Guide

PURPOSE
To promote the coping skill of exploring four triggering emotions, learning to H.A.L.T. and exploring ways to address these triggers.

POSSIBLE NAMES OF SESSIONS
- *H.A.L.T.*
- *Four emotions*
- *Coping by H.A.L.T.ing!*

BACKGROUND INFORMATION
The acronym H.A.L.T. originated in the addictions recovery literature. It stands for Hunger, Anger, Lonely, and Tired. These four emotions can be triggers to undesirable behaviors and they indicate specific needs:
- recognition of specific emotions
- encouragement to halt and problem-solve
- guidance to promote problem-solving techniques through sharing useful ideas

ACTIVITY
1. Write H.A.L.T. on the board, asking if anyone is familiar with this acronym.
2. Discuss previous knowledge and experiences with H.A.L.T.
3. Distribute handouts and pens.
4. Cover each point in the handout making sure that each emotion is discussed.
5. Ask group members to contribute realistic ideas to address these emotions.
6. Ask group members to turn their handouts over and quiz them on the words that the acronym H.A.L.T. represents.

VARIATIONS
Ask a representative from a 12-step program to speak to the group about how the coping skill of H.A.L.T. has been useful.

NOTES

Topic III — COPING SKILLS

Stressors, Coping Skills, & Supports

Getting older isn't always easy … in fact, it can be quite stressful!

Check the stressors you have experienced within the last year. List others.	Circle the letters of the coping skills that might work for you.	Circle the numbers for the people who are best able to support you in using these skills.
☐ Break-up or divorce	A. Books/movies	1. Banker/financial planner
☐ Change in activity	B. Exercise	2. Child
☐ Change of living environment	C. Focus on positives	3. Clergy
☐ Death of a loved one	D. Games/puzzles	4. Club or game members
☐ Hair/teeth/body part loss	E. Healthy routine	5. Colleague
☐ Grandchildren/children issues	F. Hobbies	6. Community resource
☐ Lack of social life	G. Leave home for awhile	7. Friend
☐ Loss of a good friend	H. Meditate	8. Grandchild
☐ Loss of income	I. Music	9. Great-grandchild
☐ Loss of a job	J. New interests	10. Group member
☐ Loss of a pet	K. Part-time work	11. Healthcare provider
☐ Mental health issues	L. Socialize	12. Long distance support
☐ Pain	M. Spend time alone	13. Neighbor
☐ Partner's loss of a job	N. Spend time in nature	14. Other relatives
☐ Physical health problem	O. Take a class	15. Partner
☐ Regrets about the past	P. Take medications	16. Social group
☐ Relative issues	Q. Talk/share	17. Social network
☐ Too much unproductive time	R. Volunteer	18. Spiritual leader
☐	S.	19.
☐	T.	20.
☐	U.	21.
☐	V.	22.
☐	W.	23.
☐	X.	24.
☐	Y.	25.
☐	Z.	26.

Stressors, Coping Skills, & Supports
Leader's Guide

PURPOSE
To assist in coping skills and support system development.

POSSIBLE NAMES OF SESSIONS
- *Life Can Be Stressful … Believe It or Not.*
- *Stress … Let's Name Names*
- *Ready or Not … Here is Some Stress*

BACKGROUND INFORMATION
Coping for senior adults can be challenging, considering the multitude of stressors and the possible lack of supports. Dealing with limited resources, society's myths of aging, and accepting limitations can be challenging. Recognizing coping skills might increase a sense of personal control and power. Identifying supports may decrease isolation and increase problem-solving successes.

ACTIVITY
1. Ask group members to identify some stressors they have experienced in the last year and write those they are willing to share on the board.
2. Distribute handouts and pens.
3. Describe activity of looking at the stressors, checking them off, and then identifying coping skills that would most likely be helpful.
4. Give group fifteen minutes to complete.
5. Share responses.
6. List all of the "other" stressors, coping skills, and supports.

VARIATIONS
1). Ask group members to identify and describe someone in their lives who has overcome adversity and how.
2) Give each group member a blank piece of paper. Instruct group members to divide the paper into three sections by folding it into thirds. Develop simple collages using pictures from magazines symbolizing stressors, coping skills, and supports.

NOTES

_____
_____
_____
_____
_____
_____
_____
_____
_____
_____
_____
_____
_____
_____
_____

Topic III — COPING SKILLS

↓	Who or what have you put (or allowed) into your life that brings you UNWANTED results?	Who or what can you put into your life that can bring you WANTED results?
People		
Food		
Daily Activities		
Drugs / Medication / Alcohol		
Other		
Other		

Recipe for Disaster – Recipe for Survival
Leader's Guide

PURPOSE
To explore the coping skills (ingredients) of knowing what factors contribute to successes and disasters.

POSSIBLE NAMES OF SESSIONS
- *What are the Key Ingredients in My Life?*
- *Cooking for Success*
- *Don't Get Burned Again!*

BACKGROUND INFORMATION
Honestly evaluating the contributing factors (or ingredients) we consciously or unconsciously put in our lives is a valuable coping skill. By looking at each category: people, daily activities, drugs, medications, alcohol, and food. Participants will present a full picture (or recipe) of how they have been living their lives. This will reveal interesting insights.

ACTIVITY
1. Make a list of factors that are sure-fire "ingredients for disaster" on the board.
   People: negative relatives, drug-using neighbors
   Food: junk food, not eating, binging
   Daily activities: watching ten hours of television a day, not getting dressed
   Drugs, alcohol, medications: couple of beers a day, not taking meds correctly
   Other: not returning phone calls, texts, or emails
2. Distribute handouts and pens.
3. Give group ten minutes to complete left side of page.
4. Share responses.
5. Discuss that recovery includes purposefully planning for success.
6. Ask group members to complete the right side of the page and discuss.
7. Share responses and support group members as they create personal recipes.

VARIATIONS
1) Write DISASTER and SURVIVAL on the board. Prepare index cards for group members to guess which category each fits in – disaster or survival. For example: Getting enough sleep, making a budget, using credit cards excessively, eating three meals a day.
2) Role play how to set appropriate boundaries to deal with "people" issues.

NOTES
_____
_____
_____
_____
_____
_____
_____
_____
_____

Topic III — COPING SKILLS

Coping Skills Journal

Today ...

I found these interactions successful: _____
_____
_____
_____
_____
_____

I found myself thinking about _____
_____
_____
_____
_____
_____

Some of the feelings I had today were _____
_____
_____
_____
_____
_____

I took good care of myself today by _____
_____
_____
_____
_____
_____

OPTIMAL WELL-BEING FOR SENIOR ADULTS II

Coping Skills Journal
Leader's Guide

PURPOSE
To reinforce coping skills by the active process of journaling and repeatedly asking the question, "How did I take care of myself today?"

POSSIBLE NAMES OF SESSIONS
- *How Do You Take Care of Yourself?*
- *Journaling to Health*
- *Dear Diary*

BACKGROUND INFORMATION
Journaling can be an effective coping skill. This coping skill journal activity focuses on four issues with a cognitive behavioral approach:
  Interactions
  Thoughts
  Feelings
  Actions

ACTIVITY
1. Introduce the need to practice coping skills for them to be effective, just like all other skill developments.
2. Distribute handouts and pens.
3. Give group members ten minutes to complete the handout for either this day or if it's early in the day, complete for the day before.
4. Discuss with emphasis on coping skill choices.
5. Distribute several additional handouts for the week.

VARIATIONS
Prepare weekly journals by photocopying several handouts and stapling them together. Issue these as clients are admitted to a program. Staff or peers can review them to support insights and coping skills.

NOTES

Topic IV

MENTAL / COGNITIVE DISORDERS

Table of Contents and Corresponding Goals for Each Section

> *The most powerful way to change someone's view is to meet them ...*
> *People who do come out and talk about mental illness,*
> *that's when healing can really begin. You can lead a productive life.*
> ~ Glenn Close

Stigma of Mental Illness 47
To increase awareness of how the stigma of mental illness still permeates society and affects individuals and families.

MOVE AWAY FROM THE MYTHS 49-56

Anxiety 49
To increase awareness of myths and facts associated with senior adults and anxiety.

Bipolar Disorder 51
To increase awareness of myths and facts associated with senior adults and bipolar disorder.

Depression 53
To increase awareness of myths and facts associated with senior adults and depression.

Dementia 55
To increase awareness of myths and facts associated with senior adults and dementia.

LEVEL OF UNDERSTANDING

 Basic Level    Intermediate Level    High Level

Topic IV — MENTAL / COGNITIVE DISORDERS

Stigma of Mental Illness

Senior adults are often reluctant to report any type of symptoms of a mental disorder because they grew up in a time when mental illness was stigmatized – and it still is to some extent!

- What movies or books contributed to the stigma of mental illness? _____
  _____
  _____
  _____

- What were you taught about people with mental illness? _____
  _____
  _____
  _____

- How has this changed over your lifetime?_____
  _____
  _____
  _____

- What famous people do you know who had or who has a mental illness? _____
  _____
  _____
  _____

- What movies or books portray the truth of mental illness? _____
  _____
  _____
  _____

- What are ways that you can be involved in breaking the barriers that people face when disclosing their mental illness to others? _____
  _____
  _____
  _____
  _____
  _____

Stigma of Mental Illness
Leader's Guide

PURPOSE
To increase awareness of how the stigma of mental illness still permeates society and affects individuals and families.

POSSIBLE NAMES OF SESSIONS
- *Stigma of Mental Illness*
- *Obstacles of Being Honest About My Mental Illness*
- *Awareness of the Stigma of Mental Illness*

BACKGROUND INFORMATION
The stigma of mental illness remains, even though it has lessened over the last few decades. It remains taboo among some people in certain cultures to disclose that one has a mental illness. There are still those who make comments, mostly out of ignorance, that are hurtful and off-putting, and influence one's ability to seek the help that is needed.

ACTIVITY
1. Write STIGMA on the board. Ask for a definition.
2. If needed, assist group members by using this definition: "Stigma is a mark of disgrace associated with a particular quality, condition, or circumstance." Discuss how the stigma of mental illness has been an obstacle to those who need help.
3. Distribute handouts.
4. Review responses.
5. Process the group by asking members: "What was brought to light in this group?"

VARIATIONS
1) Bring in a list of famous people who have recently disclosed their mental illnesses. Support their disclosures.
2) Role play different scenarios of how, when, and how much to disclose about a mental illness. Support group members in their choice of how much to disclose.

NOTES

Topic IV — MENTAL / COGNITIVE DISORDERS

MOVE AWAY FROM THE MYTHS – *Anxiety*

Our culture holds myths about senior adults and anxiety.

Complete this true and false quiz to see how much you know about anxiety.

Circle either true or false for each statement.

1. An anxiety disorder is not really an illness. . . . . T   F

2. Fainting occurs frequently with panic disorders. . . . . T   F

3. Anxiety disorders are not treatable . . . . T   F

4. Anxiety disorders are common . . . . T   F

5. Anxiety is best treated by ignoring it. . . . . T   F

6. Self-medication is an effective treatment for anxiety disorders. . . . . T   F

7. Cognitive behavioral therapy is an effective treatment for anxiety disorders . . T   F

8. Snap out of it is a good thing to say to someone experiencing anxiety . . . . T   F

9. Research on the course and treatment of anxiety in senior adults lags behind other mental health conditions, such as depression and Alzheimer's . . . . T   F

10. Loss of friends and family, decreased mobility, greater isolation, and other stressful situations can contribute to anxiety. . . . . T   F

It is important to be educated about the realities of this important topic.

Share this handout with your loved ones.

OPTIMAL WELL-BEING FOR SENIOR ADULTS II

MOVE AWAY FROM THE MYTHS – *Anxiety*
Leader's Guide

PURPOSE
To increase awareness of myths and facts about anxiety in senior adults.

POSSIBLE NAMES OF SESSIONS
- *True or False – Anxiety and Senior Adults*
- *About Anxiety*
- *Knowledge is Power: Learn About Anxiety*

BACKGROUND INFORMATION
Many people do not understand anxiety disorders. They hear myths and believe them as truths. The truth? Anxiety disorders are treatable. They do not diminish on their own. They are often under-recognized, misdiagnosed, and overlooked. It is important to educate senior adults and their loved ones about the realities of this subject for prevention and treatment.

ACTIVITY
1. Ask group members, "What is the first thing you think of when you hear the word *psychology* or *psychiatry*." Write all of the words on a flipchart or dry erase board in large print.
2. Ask group members if some of these thoughts might have prevented them from either receiving help for self or for a loved one.
3. Distribute handouts and pens.
4. Give group members ten minutes to circle the correct responses.
5. Answer key:
    1-F, 2-F, 3-F, 4-T, 5-F, 6-F, 7-T, 8-F, 9-T, 10-T

VARIATIONS
1) Educate group about distinctions between normal anxiety and anxiety disorder, including intensity and length, specific stressor(s) vs. non-specific stressor(s), other symptoms, and criteria for a medical illness.
2) Cut statements into strips and give one to each group member, one by one. Ask them to read the myth aloud and guess the answer. Then give the correct answer and discuss.
3) Arrange to have a senior adult, or a group member who successfully manages personal anxiety, come and speak to the group to describe personal experiences.

NOTES
_____
_____
_____
_____
_____
_____
_____
_____
_____
_____
_____
_____
_____

Topic IV — MENTAL / COGNITIVE DISORDERS

MOVE AWAY FROM THE MYTHS – **Bipolar Disorder**

Our culture holds myths about senior adults and bipolar disorder formerly known as manic-depression.

Complete this true and false quiz to see how much you know about bipolar disorder.

Circle either true or false for each statement.

1. Bipolar disorder symptoms *burn out* and slowly disappear with age.......... T   F

2. Untreated bipolar disorder worsens over time .... T   F

3. It is possible that people who become diagnosed as seniors had undiagnosed bipolar disorder for years.......................... T   F

4. As the population ages, the number of seniors with bipolar disorder is expected to grow .... T   F

5. Manic episodes are a normal part of aging. .... T   F

6. Common symptoms of bipolar disorder include distractibility, confusion, and hyperactivity........................... T   F

7. Bipolar disorder symptoms can appear as a side effect of certain medications .... T   F

8. People who have symptoms of bipolar disorder need a full medical work up . T   F

9. Treatment of a senior with bipolar disorder is more complicated than treatment of a young person .... T   F

10. *Talk Therapy* is not useful for people with bipolar disorder. .... T   F

It is important to be educated about the realities of this important topic.

Share this handout with your loved ones.

OPTIMAL WELL-BEING FOR SENIOR ADULTS II

MOVE AWAY FROM THE MYTHS – **Bipolar Disorder**
Leader's Guide

PURPOSE
To increase awareness of myths and facts about bipolar disorder in senior adults.

POSSIBLE NAMES OF SESSIONS
- What do you know about Bipolar Disorder and Senior Adults?
- Manic Depression or Bipolar?
- Knowledge is Power: Bipolar and Seniors

BACKGROUND INFORMATION
Many people do not understand bipolar disorders. They hear myths and believe them as truths. The best way of exploring the facts can be done in a group setting to allow group members to support new learning.

ACTIVITY
1. Ask group members, "What is the first thing you think of when you hear the word *psychology* or *psychiatry*." Write all of the words on a flipchart or dry erase board in large print.
2. Ask group members if some of these thoughts might have prevented them from either receiving help for self or for a loved one.
3. Distribute handouts and pens.
4. Give group members ten minutes to circle the correct responses.
5. Answer key:
   1-F, 2-T, 3-T, 4-T, 5-F, 6-T, 7-T, 8-T, 9-T, 10-F

VARIATIONS
1) Find a list of famous people who have or had bipolar disorder. Discuss that people with bipolar disorder can be creative geniuses; unfortunately their lives can be filled with suffering.
2) Cut statements into strips and give one to each group member, one by one. Ask them to read the myth aloud and guess the answer. Then give the correct answer and discuss.
3) Arrange to have a senior adult or group member who is successfully managing personal bipolar disorder, come and speak to the group to describe personal experiences.

NOTES
_____
_____
_____
_____
_____
_____
_____
_____
_____
_____
_____
_____

Topic IV — MENTAL / COGNITIVE DISORDERS

MOVE AWAY FROM THE MYTHS – *Depression*

Our culture holds myths about senior adults and depression.

Complete this true and false quiz to see how much you know about bipolar disorder.

Circle either true or false for each statement.

1. Senior adults often deny a depression. . . . . T   F

2. Memory complaints and bodily complaints can be signs of depression . . . . . . T   F

3. Hearing loss may be a contributing factor to depression . . . . T   F

4. A depressed mood is the same thing as a clinical depression. . . . . T   F

5. Depression does not frequently occur with other medical illnesses. . . . . T   F

6. Depression is not a significant predictor of suicide in senior adults. . . . . T   F

7. A first depression of a senior adult may be his or her last . . . . T   F

8. Depression is a normal part of aging . . . . T   F

9. Changes in sleeping habits and appetite can be signs of depression . . . . T   F

10. Suicide rates in later life are high. . . . . T   F

It is important to be educated about the realities of this important topic.

Share this handout with your loved ones.

OPTIMAL WELL-BEING FOR SENIOR ADULTS II

MOVE AWAY FROM THE MYTHS – *Depression*
Leader's Guide

PURPOSE
To increase awareness of myths and facts about depression in senior adults.

POSSIBLE NAMES OF SESSIONS
- *Keeping Up-To-Date*
- *TRUE or FALSE – Depression in Older Adults*
- *Depression – Is It Significant in Senior Adults?*

BACKGROUND INFORMATION
Many people have fears about depression and mental illness. They hear myths and believe them as truths. The reality is that depression is treatable. It is often under-recognized and overlooked. It is important to educate senior adults and their loved ones about the reality of this topic for prevention and treatment.

ACTIVITY
1. Ask group members, "What is the first thing you think of when you hear the word *psychology* or *psychiatry*." Write all of the words on a flipchart or dry erase board in large print.
2. Ask group members if some of these thoughts might have prevented them from either receiving help for self or for a loved one.
3. Distribute handouts and pens.
4. Give group members ten minutes to circle the correct responses.
5. Answer key:
   1-T, 2-T, 3-T, 4-F, 5-F, 6-F, 7-T, 8-F, 9-T, 10-T

VARIATIONS
1) Educate the group about distinctions between depressed mood and clinical depression, including intensity, length, other symptoms, and meeting criteria for a mental illness.
2) Cut myths into strips and give one to each group member, one by one. Ask them to read myth aloud and guess the answer. Then give the correct answer and discuss.
3) Arrange to have a senior adult or a group member who is successfully managing personal depression, come and speak to the group to describe personal experiences.

NOTES

Topic IV — MENTAL / COGNITIVE DISORDERS

MOVE AWAY FROM THE MYTHS – *Dementia*

Our culture holds myths about senior adults and dementia.
For family members to be supportive, it is important that they
have accurate information about this illness.
In this way, realistic expectations, good decisions,
and compassion can be fostered.

Complete this true and false quiz to see how much you know about bipolar disorder.

Circle either true or false for each statement.

1. There is only one kind of dementia. . . . .   T   F

2. People with dementia frequently have trouble communicating . . . .   T   F

3. Dementia is a progressive disease. . . . .   T   F

4. Once a person is diagnosed with dementia, there is nothing
   that can be done . . . .   T   F

5. It is best to correct a person with dementia when the person says
   something incorrect. . . . .   T   F

6. There is no cure for dementia.. . . . .   T   F

7. If a person has dementia, that means the person is not competent. . . . .   T   F

8. Dementia symptoms can vary hour to hour . . . .   T   F

9. Dementia always results in aggression and violence . . . .   T   F

10. Structure, love, and safety are important aspects of high
    quality dementia care. . . . .   T   F

It is important to be educated about the realities of this important topic.

Share this handout with your loved ones.

OPTIMAL WELL-BEING FOR SENIOR ADULTS II

MOVE AWAY FROM THE MYTHS – *Dementia*
Leader's Guide

PURPOSE
To increase awareness of myths and facts about dementia in senior adults.

POSSIBLE NAMES OF SESSIONS
- *Families Deserve the Truth*
- *Knowing the Facts About Dementia*
- *Dementia: It's A Disease*

BACKGROUND INFORMATION
The myths associated with dementia are scary – both for the person with dementia – and for the family. It is best to present this information in a family support group or a family education group, with or without the person with dementia, depending on the level of dementia and the circumstances involved. Group members with mild dementia will benefit from this activity with or without family members present.

ACTIVITY
1. Explain that knowledge is power.
2. Introduce the topic of dementia as *sensitive, emotional*, and even *scary*.
3. Distribute handouts and pens, and complete together offering information that is brief and concise, honest and direct, yet supportive to the group.
4. Focus on number 10, offering details of how to provide structure, love, and safety.
5. Answer key: 1-F, 2-T, 3-T, 4-F, 5-F, 6-T, 7-F, 8-T, 9-F, 10-T

VARIATIONS
Offer helpful local or national resources such as home health, caregivers' listing for respite, day programs, and support groups for the person with dementia and for the person's caregiver(s).

NOTES

Topic V
POSITIVE ATTITUDE
Table of Contents and Corresponding Goals for Each Section

A positive attitude is not going to save you. What it's going to do is, every day, between now and the day you die, whether that's a short time from now or a long time from now, that every day, you're going to actually live.

~ Elizabeth Edwards

What Makes You Joyous and Satisfied? 59
To determine what factors in our lives play a role in finding joy and meaning.
To see the positive side of life and nurture an attitude of gratitude.
To determine what might be lacking in one's life.

Cultivating Gratitude 61
To promote an attitude of gratitude using a variety of gratitude exercises.

Slow and Steady Wins the Race 63
To set daily, weekly, and monthly goals to keep moving in a positive direction.

Same Old, Same Old? Not for Long! 65
To increase positive and meaningful lifestyle activities.

A Love Letter to Me 67
To nurture the spiritual side of ourselves to develop and / or maintain a positive self-image.

LEVEL OF UNDERSTANDING

 Basic Level    Intermediate Level    High Level

Topic V — POSITIVE ATTITUDE

What Makes You Joyous and Satisfied?

Put your first name in the center of the flower under Self.
Fill in the eight petals with whatever makes you *joyous* and *satisfied*.

OPTIMAL WELL-BEING FOR SENIOR ADULTS II

What Makes You Joyous and Satisfied?
Leader's Guide

PURPOSE
To determine what factors in our lives play a role in finding joy and meaning.

To see the positive side of life and nurture an attitude of gratitude.

To determine what might be lacking in one's life.

POSSIBLE NAMES OF SESSIONS
- *Flower Power*
- *Contentment Counts*
- *To Bloom and Grow*

BACKGROUND INFORMATION
Past events along with life experiences, personal talents, and cultural differences, are only a few factors that influence how we define what promotes joy and satisfaction in our lives. Analyzing one's life in the here and now is a valuable experience.

ACTIVITY
1. Distribute handouts and pens or markers. Write on the board: "What makes you joyous and satisfied?" Distribute handouts and explain that this session will focus on YOU as an individual.
2. Ask group members to begin this activity by putting their first name in the line under SELF in the center of the flower.
3. Instruct group members to fill in the eight petals with whatever makes them joyous and / or satisfied. Examples include: family, love, accomplishments, job, health, travel, freedom, owning a home, financial security, education, community, friends, meeting a goal, etc.
4. Emphasize that there are no right or wrong answers and that responses will vary.
5. Share responses.
6. Process, using any combination of comments / questions below, or develop your own:
   a. Discuss the idea that we are all unique; our family and life experiences have made us unique.
      What has been a positive experience for you that influenced one of your answers?
   b. Discuss how we are each like flowers. We bloom and develop in our own time and way.
      What type of flower are you? A slow-to-open rose, or a very quick-to-open daisy?
   c. Observe the flower drawing carefully. Each petal is a little different. It is not a perfect flower.
      Is anything in nature actually perfect? Each creation is unique and special. What is the most unique part of your flower? Explain.
   d. Do you look at others as being like that flower, each one unique and special? Tell us about someone you know who can be compared to a flower. Explain.
   e. Is there someone in your life who has helped you to flower and grow? How has that person cultivated you? Who is this person? How did this person effect you?
   f. Is there part of your flower that has not developed yet? Explain
   g. How can you be a positive influence for others so they may grow?

VARIATIONS
1) Introduce group with the following ice-breaker. Write four words on the board: health, money, fame, and love. Ask group members to choose only one word to answer this question: Which would make you the most joyous and most satisfied? Discuss.
2) Create "Attitudes of Gratitude" journals, using the chosen petal themes for starters: I am grateful that I have my _____.
I feel satisfied because _____.

NOTES
_____
_____

Topic V — POSITIVE ATTITUDE

Cultivating Gratitude

Gratitude: being mindfully aware of the tremendously supportive and positive energy that allows me to be in the flow of wellness and wholeness.

IDEAS TO CULTIVATE GRATITUDE

1. **Listen** to spirit-filled music.
   Allow the music to remind you of what is important and valuable in your life.

2. **Walk** with gratitude on your mind.
   Take a short or long walk in nature. Allow the natural world to move you to a place of wonder and awe.

3. **Compose** a list of things for which you are grateful.
   Consider different categories: things, people, and experiences.

4. **Journal** daily.
   Use prompts such as …
   What or who inspired me today?
   or
   What was the best moment I had today?

5. **Write** 52 thank you notes a year, and send them.
   Once a week, notice people you can thank and let them know.

6. Other _____
   _____

7. Other _____
   _____

Never let things you want make you forget the things you have!
~ Author Unknown

Cultivating Gratitude
Leader's Guide

PURPOSE
To promote an attitude of gratitude using a variety of gratitude exercises.

POSSIBLE NAMES OF SESSIONS
- *Gratitude*
- *Me and My Gratitude*
- *365 Days of Thanks Giving*

BACKGROUND INFORMATION
Cultivating gratitude implies an active process that one engages in to achieve a "grateful state." It is impossible to feel grateful for every moment of every day, but it is a worthwhile effort to feel grateful each day, even for a moment.

ACTIVITY
1. Write the quote from the bottom of the handout onto the board: "Never let the things you want make you forget the things you have!"
2. Give each group member time to reflect and then share.
3. Distribute handouts and pens.
4. Review each point on the handout. Ask for comments / examples along the way.
5. Give five minutes for group members to complete #3 on the back of the handout. Share responses if time allows.
6. Complete session emphasizing this action-oriented practice focusing on the underlined verbs.

VARIATIONS
Use inspirational quotes or verses that will be within the group's grasp to promote gratitude. Place on a unit board or flyer. If possible, use the quotations as a prompt for discussions, journaling, artwork, and relaxation sessions, etc.

NOTES

Topic V — POSITIVE ATTITUDE

S L O W and STEADY Wins the Race

**Remember the story of the tortoise and the hare?
The tortoise won … with determination, persistence,
and an I-can-do-it attitude!**

Realistic goals keep us moving in positive directions, towards good health, the ability to do what we want to do, and choices of when and how we want to act. Sharing our goals with others encourages specific goal-setting and accountability, which can help us stick to the goals. Complete the following sentences.

By the end of the day, I will _____

_____

I will share this goal with _____

By the end of the week, I will _____

_____

I will share this goal with _____

By the end of the month, I will _____

_____

I will share this goal with _____

S L O W and STEADY Wins the Race
Leader's Guide

PURPOSE
To set daily, weekly, and monthly goals to keep us moving in a positive direction.

POSSIBLE NAMES OF SESSIONS
- *Keeping on Going*
- *Sharing the Goal!*
- *Daily, Weekly, and Monthly Goals*

BACKGROUND INFORMATION
Goals can further our intentions. We often think we want to do something – sometimes we tell someone, and sometimes we don't. Sometimes, stating a goal can make the action come alive. Including supportive people in the goals we set can elicit the help to accomplish those goals, improve relationships, and reduce possible isolation.

ACTIVITY
1. Write on the board all of the possible areas in which we can set goals; e.g., eating, caring for our bodies, housekeeping, pursuing, maintaining, and nourishing relationships, making calls, engaging in satisfying activities, and reducing possible isolation.
2. Explain that a goal is an action that can be written and crossed off when accomplished (not a dream that can't be crossed off).
3. Distribute handouts and pens.
4. Give one or two examples of goals and people with whom we can share those goals.
   Example:
   By the end of the day I will call my sister. I can share this goal with my neighbor.
   I will clean my bedroom right after dinner. I can share this goal with my case manager.
5. Give group members ten minutes to develop personal goals.
6. Share in groups of three or four. Ask group members to support each other with positive feedback.
7. Ask group members to share their favorite goals and list them on the board.

VARIATIONS
1) Develop a way of checking with group members to see if goals were accomplished. (Notebook, flipchart, journal, etc.)
2) Discuss the possibility of checking with group members to see if goals were accomplished and bring rewards to individuals or group if appropriate. List effective self-rewards.

NOTES

_____
_____
_____
_____
_____
_____
_____
_____
_____

Topic V — POSITIVE ATTITUDE

Same Old, Same Old? Not for Long!

Although there is great value to keeping a daily routine, life can become boring, stale, and predictable. Change can be good, and it helps us to be fun and interesting people.

Read below and check three or more activities that appeal to you. Add in any of your own. Then complete the second column by answering who could be helpful and/or supportive. Next, in the third column, write the next step in doing this new activity.

New Activity	Who Could Be Helpful and/or Supportive?	What's the Next Step In Doing This?
☐ Become involved in politics		
☐ Engage in a new sport or exercise		
☐ Get together with a new friend		
☐ Go to a new place in your community		
☐ Join a club		
☐ Take a course or class		
☐ Travel		
☐ Try a new food		
☐ Volunteer		
☐ Other		
☐ Other		

Same Old, Same Old? Not for Long!
Leader's Guide

PURPOSE
To increase positive meaningful and lifestyle activities.

POSSIBLE NAMES OF SESSIONS
- *Keep It Interesting*
- *All Work and No Play …*
- *Ready for a Challenge?*

BACKGROUND INFORMATION
People may have a tendency to stick to old routines and expectations, which in turn may lead to rigid routines and inflexibility. Oftentimes, the result is boredom, isolation, and a depressed mood. New activities may introduce a new social group, provide exciting challenges, offer different ideas and elicit interesting conversations! In addition, it may take the place of sedentary or nonproductive activities.

ACTIVITY
1. Introduce concept by reviewing background information. It might be helpful to elicit a sense of the group members' activity level by asking thought-provoking questions.
   Examples:
   "How many hours of television do you watch a day?"
   "When was the last time you tried a new food?"
2. Distribute handouts and pens.
3. Ask a group member to read the top two paragraphs aloud.
4. Give group members ten minutes to complete the handouts.
5. Briefly review results by asking who checked which item in the list.
6. Pair group members of similar interests to discuss plans for five minutes.
7. Reconvene and ask group members to share interesting plans and ideas.

VARIATIONS
1) Develop goals, accountability, and a method for reporting back to the group the progress that has been made.
2) Bring a new food (easy snack, exotic fruit, etc.) to the group as an intro and process the results.
3) Bring in carryout menus of newer restaurants, brochures with newer community programs, and any other local resource that may be overlooked or under-utilized, for group members to see.

NOTES

Topic V — POSITIVE ATTITUDE

A Love Letter to Me

**Being mindful to love ourselves no matter what requires effort.
We must refute past and present negative messages
and replace those with loving, encouraging, and nurturing messages.**

I, resolve to love myself as a unique individual in this world who _____
_____
_____
_____
_____

Some things that I have going for me are my _____
_____
_____
_____

There is just one me – and I resolve that one spiritual pursuit I can adopt right now is to embrace this person called ME.

Which people allow me to embrace myself as unique and worthy of love? _____
_____
_____
_____
_____

What actions allow me to embrace myself as unique and worthy of love? _____
_____
_____
_____

What negative influences or attitudes can I limit to overcome that power in my life? _____
_____
_____
_____
_____

OPTIMAL WELL-BEING FOR SENIOR ADULTS II

A Love Letter to Me
Leader's Guide

PURPOSE
To nurture the spiritual side of ourselves to develop or maintain a positive self-image.

POSSIBLE NAMES OF SESSIONS
- *Loving Myself*
- *Seeking the Spiritual Side*
- *I Am Worth It!*

BACKGROUND INFORMATION
It is rare to be able to create opportunities to talk about how we feel about ourselves in an open and supportive atmosphere. The nature of spirituality is that it attempts to connect us with our personal uniqueness that we are as human beings. Spiritual access to a positive self-image might be a natural 'way in' for some seniors.

ACTIVITY
1. Discuss obstacles or barriers in developing or maintaining a positive self-image.
2. Distribute handouts and pens, markers, colored pencils, or watercolors.
3. Read the handout aloud and then give group members ten minutes to complete.
4. Ask the following:
   a. Which was the easiest part of the love letter to complete? The most difficult?
   b. What were some actions or activities that allow group members to embrace themselves as unique and worthy of love.
5. Divide group into pairs to pursue discussion of how to encourage a positive self-image.
6. Reconvene and encourage pairs to share their best ideas.

VARIATIONS
1) Brainstorm a list of ways the facility can be more supportive in helping to assure that clients' spiritual needs are met. Share the list with people who can make things happen.
2) Offer participants an opportunity to be expressive and creative. Place markers, watercolors, colored pencils, etc., on the table. Instruct participants to use the back of their handout to complete one of these sentences:
   "Other spiritual pursuits that sound interesting to me right now are _____."
   or
   "Ways for me to stay positive are _____."
   Ask them to depict their ideas in images or drawings rather than words. Play soft background music. Share in a supportive atmosphere. Explore the role that art, music, and poetry might have in self-image and spirituality.

NOTES
_____
_____
_____
_____
_____
_____

Topic VI

RELATIONSHIPS

Table of Contents and Corresponding Goals for Each Section

> *In human relationships, kindness and lies are worth a thousand truths.*
> ~ Graham Greene

How to Make a Friend 71
To explore the steps it takes to make friends.

Word Search for Healthy Relationships 73
To explore the characteristics of healthy relationships.

Developing Meaningful Relationships 75
To promote deepening of friendships through conscious actions.

SEVEN DATING GUIDELINES 77
To explore safe dating guidelines.

Learn About Elder Abuse and Neglect 79
To educate anyone who is interested in information about elder abuse and neglect.

LEVEL OF UNDERSTANDING

 Basic Level  Intermediate Level  High Level

Topic VI — RELATIONSHIPS

How to Make a Friend

The road to a friend's house is never long.

~ A Danish Proverb

OPTIMAL WELL-BEING FOR SENIOR ADULTS II

How to Make a Friend
Leader's Guide

PURPOSE

To explore the steps it takes to make friends.

POSSIBLE NAMES OF SESSIONS
- *Never Too Late to Make Friends*
- *That's What Friends are For*
- *Ya Gotta Have Friends*

BACKGROUND INFORMATION

Research indicates that as we age, we often have fewer opportunities for meeting new people and developing relationships. Friendships can provide a tremendous source of satisfaction, support, and interest to one's life. Friends can be a very positive force in weathering life's storms. Friends can share fond memories and be a valuable sounding board in ways that family sometimes cannot.

ACTIVITY

1. Distribute handouts and pens.
2. Discuss background information and receive group input about the meaning and value of friends, especially as one grows older.
3. Instruct group members to write on the blank steps the values of making a friend.
4. Offer examples such as talk, listen, bake, write, send a card, call, say a kind word, smile, join groups, invite someone over, etc.
5. Share completed handouts. Discuss similar and different responses. Discuss the challenges in making and keeping friends as we get older.
6. Discuss any of these:
   a. What does it mean to be a 'good friend'?
   b. What do you like doing by yourself?
   c. What activities do you like to share with others?
   d. If you could have one friend to do something really special with you, what would you do together?.

VARIATIONS

1) List mottos, expressions, or sayings that speak of friends or relationships.
   Example: "Make new friends but keep the old, one is silver and the other's gold."
   "A friend in need is a friend indeed."
   "Fair-weather friend."
   "Like ships that pass in the night."
   "The Golden Rule."
2) Discuss and list ways that people in the group could likely meet new friends.

NOTES

_____
_____
_____
_____
_____
_____
_____

Topic VI — RELATIONSHIPS

Healthy Relationships WORD SEARCH

Look for these words below.
(Not only for this word search, but in your various relationships!)
They can be vertical, horizontal, diagonal, forward, backward, or upside-down

Accept	Consent	Kind	Respect
Assertive	Considerate	Listen	Share
Boundaries	Dignity	Love	Speak Up
Common Interest	Forgive	Laugh	Support
Compassion	Give And Take	Mutual	Tolerant
Compromise	Grateful	Open Communications	Trust

I	N	T	E	R	E	T	C	O	M	T	O	L	E	R	A	N	T	S	P
A	D	G	J	L	M	A	R	C	S	U	V	O	N	A	N	O	O	N	E
Z	O	O	A	O	O	R	L	O	I	N	A	V	D	N	I	T	U	O	R
B	C	O	M	M	O	N	I	N	T	E	R	E	S	T	S	F	H	I	S
V	O	T	R	E	L	E	S	S	O	R	E	N	I	S	L	O	G	T	N
E	N	T	W	A	K	E	T	E	L	A	S	U	P	P	O	R	T	A	O
T	S	U	R	T	B	I	E	N	E	R	P	F	P	O	C	G	I	C	S
H	I	V	I	O	W	O	N	T	I	F	E	B	I	T	A	I	C	I	G
I	D	I	G	N	I	T	Y	D	L	O	C	A	G	R	L	V	E	N	I
N	E	B	J	U	M	B	E	L	K	A	T	E	T	E	L	E	A	U	V
B	R	C	O	M	P	A	S	S	I	O	N	M	C	A	H	U	M	M	E
G	A	S	H	U	T	X	H	L	V	R	O	I	U	N	S	E	D	M	A
G	T	I	M	E	N	P	E	U	Y	E	W	G	E	T	R	Y	L	O	N
C	E	D	M	I	N	D	F	I	S	K	H	E	R	M	U	P	A	C	D
L	A	K	E	N	B	E	A	N	R	T	U	K	T	A	L	A	N	N	T
E	H	A	R	D	S	H	A	R	E	E	J	G	O	A	T	R	L	E	A
M	A	T	I	A	H	A	N	E	I	A	L	D	P	P	Z	E	I	P	K
E	P	H	T	L	U	R	A	C	C	E	P	T	I	E	A	B	F	O	E
N	E	Y	C	O	M	P	R	O	M	I	S	E	S	P	E	A	K	U	P
E	S	T	E	R	E	V	I	T	R	E	S	S	A	K	A	T	H	Y	L

OPTIMAL WELL-BEING FOR SENIOR ADULTS II

Healthy Relationships WORD SEARCH
Leader's Guide

PURPOSE
To explore the characteristics of healthy relationships.

POSSIBLE NAMES OF SESSIONS
- *Looking for Healthy Relationships*
- *What are the Components of a Healthy Relationship?*
- *Functional Relationships vs. Dysfunctional Relationships*

BACKGROUND INFORMATION
Too often we find ourselves in relationships that compromise our well-being. Sometimes these relationships are long-standing and the onset of the dysfunction has come on slowly. Other times, they are newer relationships and we can easily look back and see how and where the dysfunction appeared. Exploring the characteristics of healthy relationships allows one to evaluate what is present or absent in current relationships and how functional or dysfunctional they are.

ACTIVITY
1. Ask group members to identify characteristics of healthy relationships. Write them on the board.
2. Inform group members that the items on the board are what we are looking for in our relationships.
3. Distribute handouts and pens or highlighters.
4. Give group members ten minutes to complete.
5. Ask group members to identify which are the top three characteristics that they have in their lives, and which characteristics they would benefit from having more of in their lives.

VARIATIONS
Explore "crucial conversations" that need to occur with group members and their friends or families to facilitate healthier relationships.

I	N	T	E	R	E	T	C	O	M	T	O	L	E	R	A	N	T	S	P
A	D	G	J	M	A	R	C	C	S	U	V	O	N	A	N	O	O	N	E
Z	O	O	A	O	O	R	L	O	I	N	A	V	D	N	I	T	U	O	R
B	C	O	M	M	O	N	I	N	T	E	R	E	S	T	S	F	H	I	S
V	O	T	R	E	L	E	S	S	O	R	E	N	I	S	L	O	G	T	N
E	N	T	W	A	K	E	T	E	L	A	S	U	P	P	O	R	T	A	O
T	S	U	R	T	B	I	E	N	E	R	P	F	P	O	C	G	I	C	S
H	I	V	I	O	W	O	N	T	I	F	E	B	I	T	A	I	C	I	G
I	D	I	G	N	I	T	Y	D	L	O	C	A	G	R	L	V	E	N	I
N	E	B	J	U	M	B	E	L	K	A	T	E	T	E	L	E	A	U	V
B	R	C	O	M	P	A	S	S	I	O	N	M	C	A	H	U	M	M	E
G	A	S	H	U	T	X	H	L	V	R	O	I	K	N	S	E	D	M	A
G	T	I	M	E	N	P	E	U	Y	E	W	G	E	T	R	Y	L	O	N
C	E	D	M	I	N	D	F	I	S	K	H	E	R	M	U	P	A	C	D
L	A	K	E	N	B	E	A	N	R	T	U	K	T	A	L	A	N	N	T
E	H	A	R	D	S	H	A	R	E	E	J	G	O	A	T	R	L	E	A
M	A	T	I	A	H	A	N	E	I	A	L	D	P	P	Z	E	I	P	K
E	P	H	T	L	U	R	A	C	C	E	P	T	I	E	A	B	F	O	E
N	E	Y	C	O	M	P	R	O	M	I	S	E	S	P	E	A	K	U	P
E	S	T	E	R	E	V	I	T	R	E	S	S	A	K	A	T	H	Y	L

NOTES
_____
_____
_____
_____
_____

Topic VI — RELATIONSHIPS

Developing Meaningful Relationships

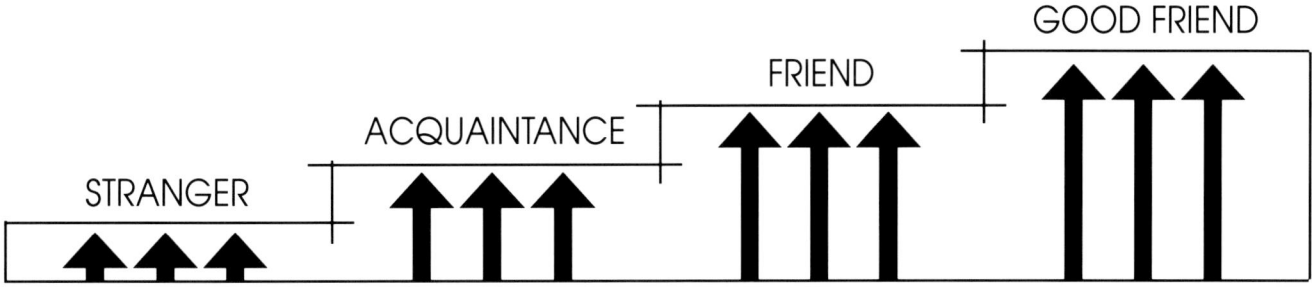

This handout focuses on the process of how to develop more meaningful relationships. Most of us have many strangers and acquaintances in our lives but few friends and very few good friends. It can be challenging as we get older to make and keep friends as people either move away, we move away, or unfortunately, people die. The need for having and being good friends is vital for healthful living.

What I'm Not Doing	Possible Obstacles	Alternative Ideas or Ways Around the Obstacles
Example: Inviting people over	Apartment is too small	Use outdoor space or invite one or two people at a time
Inviting people over.		
Joining a group or club.		
Going on an outing with someone.		

What I Have Noticed	Possible Reasons	Alternative Ideas or Ways Around the Reasons
Example: People don't seem to be interested in me.	I talk about my health problems a lot	Ask people what is happening in their lives. Tell them about something fun I have been doing.
People don't seem to be interested in me.		
People don't invite me over or call me.		
I don't feel included.		

OPTIMAL WELL-BEING FOR SENIOR ADULTS II

Developing Meaningful Relationships
Leader's Guide

PURPOSE
To promote deepening of relationships through conscious actions.

POSSIBLE NAMES OF SESSIONS
- *From Stranger to Good Friend*
- *Meaningful Relationships*
- *Taking Friendships to the Next Level*

BACKGROUND INFORMATION
Senior adults describe feeling lonely and isolated, especially when the subject of depression and aging occurs. People also describe the challenge of having meaningful conversations vs. superficial ones. This handout serves as a framework for looking at this issue and supporting the process of deepening friendships.

ACTIVITY
1. Explore the issue of superficial relationships. Ask group members to describe a superficial relationship. Explain to group members that an abundance of superficial relationships and a lack of more meaningful relationships can result in social isolation.
2. Distribute handouts and pens.
3. Review the top section of the handout.
4. Proceed with creative problem solving for alternative ideas or ways around the obstacle in the first example.
5. Give group members five minutes to complete the top section of the handout.
6. Proceed with creative problem solving for alternate ideas or ways around the possible reasons at the bottom of the handout in the second example.
7. Give group members five minutes to complete the bottom section of the handout.
8. Review completed handouts facilitating possible actions and problem solving.

VARIATIONS
1) Openly discuss fear of loneliness and isolation as clear and present dangers of aging.
2) Discuss undesirable behaviors which may alienate others and contribute to social isolation and loneliness, e.g., talking excessively about physical issues, complaining, negative attitudes, etc.

NOTES
_____
_____
_____
_____
_____
_____
_____
_____
_____
_____

Topic VI — RELATIONSHIPS

SEVEN DATING GUIDELINES

Senior adults are finding themselves dating more and more. There are many ways for seniors to meet people to date: friends, social events, blind dates, internet dating sites, and chatrooms.

Seven dating guidelines - reminders of how to be safe and smart:

1. Arrange to meet in a public place with a well-lit parking lot vs. either of your homes.

Your thoughts, experiences, and/or ideas: _____
_____

2. Use your own transportation vs. driving together.

Your thoughts, experiences, and/or ideas: _____
_____

3. Ask simple and direct questions. If the person will not answer you, this person may have something to hide.

Your thoughts, experiences, and/or ideas: _____
_____

4. Avoid alcohol. It lessons inhibitions. If you do take a drink, never leave it unattended.

Your thoughts, experiences, and/or ideas: _____
_____

5. Be careful about how much personal information you disclose.

Your thoughts, experiences, and/or ideas: _____
_____

6. If you choose to use an internet dating service, check out the privacy policy to avoid your personal information being posted. Do not use your real name, home or email address, or phone number, on your profile.

Your thoughts, experiences, and/or ideas: _____
_____

7. If you have any type of a bad feeling about someone, trust your instincts. Do not respond to questions or requests for money.

Your thoughts, experiences, and/or ideas: _____
_____

OPTIMAL WELL-BEING FOR SENIOR ADULTS II

SEVEN DATING GUIDELINES
Leader's Guide

PURPOSE
To explore safe dating guidelines.

POSSIBLE NAMES OF SESSIONS
- *Me? Date?*
- *Safety in Dating*
- *Date? It's worth a Try!*

BACKGROUND INFORMATION
More and more, senior adults are finding themselves single due to divorce rates and people living longer. Although the majority of dates in the senior population are safe, there are reasons to be cautious. Following the seven provided guidelines will reduce the fears and the avoidance of dating.

ACTIVITY
1. Write on the board: "What are your fears about dating?"
2. Discuss responses validating their fears.
3. Distribute handouts and pens.
4. Review the handout together as a group with appropriate sharing and discussion about members' thoughts of each of the seven guidelines.
5. Discuss benefits of dating.

VARIATIONS
1) Research popular online dating internet sites to illustrate points covered.
2) Have a discussion about the pros and cons of dating.

NOTES

Topic VI — RELATIONSHIPS

Learn About Elder Abuse and Neglect

Fill in the blanks using the key words in the box below.

WHAT IS ELDER ABUSE?

1) It is when _____ are harmed in some substantial way, often by people who are directly responsible for their _____.

WHO IS LIKELY TO BE ABUSED?

Factors that influence an individual for being at greater risk for abuse:

2) Dementia

3) Social _____

4) Severe illness

5) History of domestic _____

WHERE DOES ABUSE OCCUR?

6) Elder abuse most often takes place where the elder _____.

7) Most often in the home where the _____ are family members.

WHAT ARE THE TYPES OF ELDER ABUSE?

8) Healthcare _____ and abuse

9) Emotional

10) Neglect by caregivers or _____-_____.

11) Physical

12) Financial _____

13) Sexual

WHAT CAN I DO TO PREVENT ELDER ABUSE AND NEGLECT?

14) If you are the caregiver, explore support, _____, _____-_____ practices.

15) If you feel vulnerable to being abused and/or neglected, enlist _____ help, avoid isolation, and speak up to someone you _____.

KEY WORDS

| abusers | care | exploitation | fraud | isolation | legal | lives |
| respite | self-neglect | seniors | stress-reduction | trust | violence | |

Learn About Elder Abuse and Neglect
Leader's Guide

PURPOSE
To educate anyone who is interested in information about elder abuse and neglect.

POSSIBLE NAMES OF SESSIONS
- *Be in the Know, NOW!*
- *Elder Abuse and Neglect*
- *What to Do About Elder Abuse*

BACKGROUND INFORMATION
Elder abuse and neglect is unfortunately on the rise. Both the demands of caregiving and the needs of the elderly can create situations in which abuse is more likely to occur. Open conversations and education can support prevention.

ACTIVITY
1. Write ELDER ABUSE and NEGLECT on the board. Ask group members what they know about this topic.
2. Distribute handouts and pens.
3. Review each section and allow group members to fill in the blanks. Assist them in finding the correct answers as needed.
4. Research with the group members the local and/or national hotline phone numbers to contact if one is suspected of elder abuse or neglect.

KEY WORDS
1) seniors; care
3) isolation
5) violence
6) lives
7) abusers
8) fraud
10) self-neglect
12) exploitation
14) respite & stress-reduction
15) legal & trust

VARIATIONS
Expand on the types of elder abuse, using examples the group is aware of, or use local clippings from the newspaper or magazines.

NOTES

Topic VII
RESILIENCY
Table of Contents and Corresponding Goals for Each Section

Resiliency isn't a single skill. It's a variety of skills and coping mechanisms. To bounce back from bumps in the road as well as failures ...
~ Jean Chatzky

What Does Being Resilient Look Like? ... 83
To explore the basic characteristics of being resilient.

RESILIENCY: 85-92

Enjoy, Explore, & Experiment 85
To pursue being actively engaged in three resilient characteristics: enjoying, experimenting, and exploring.

Imagine, Innovate, & Invent 87
To pursue being actively engaged in three resilient characteristics: imagining, innovating, and inventing.

Take It to the Limit 89
To pursue being actively engaged in fortifying resiliency by learning to take it to the limit.

Involve Self in the Greater Good 91
To pursue being actively engaged in fortifying resiliency by involving self in the greater good.

LEVEL OF UNDERSTANDING
Basic Level | Intermediate Level | High Level

Topic VII — RESILIENCY

What Does Being Resilient Look Like?

- **R** - Rebounding from adversity
- **E** - Experiencing life to its fullest
- **S** - Supporting and receiving support
- **I** - Involving self in the greater good
- **L** - Living in the moment
- **I** - Imagining, innovating, and inventing
- **E** - Enjoying, experimenting, and exploring
- **N** - Not giving up or giving in needlessly
- **T** - Taking it to the limit

**Fostering your resiliency will contribute to your healthy aging process.
Being resilient incorporates many daily mind and body practices.**

Describe one person you know who demonstrates at least one characteristic listed above. Explain.

_____

_____

_____

> *When one door of happiness closes, another opens; but often we look so long at the closed door that we do not see the one that has been opened for us.*
>
> ~ Helen Keller

OPTIMAL WELL-BEING FOR SENIOR ADULTS II

What Does Being Resilient Look Like?
Leader's Guide

PURPOSE

To explore the basic characteristics of being resilient.

POSSIBLE NAMES OF SESSIONS
- *Fostering Resiliency*
- *Be Resilient*
- *Resiliency for Life!*

BACKGROUND INFORMATION

Resiliency is a popular and empowering topic. Being able to take what life throws our way and *weather the storm* is a very desirable way to age. Cultivating resilient characteristics is broken down into four additional handouts in this chapter.
1. *Enjoy, Explore, & Experiment*, page 85.
2. *Imagine, Innovate, & Invent*, page 87.
3. *Take It to the Limit*, page 89.
4. *Involve Self in the Greater Good*, page 91.

ACTIVITY
1. Define resilient as *able to withstand or recover quickly from difficulty*; or develop a definition with the group.
2. Distribute handouts. Read and discuss each characteristic.
3. Ask the group to research famous people who exemplify characteristics of being resilient.
   (Examples: Helen Keller, Mahatma Gandhi, Abraham Lincoln, Oprah Winfrey)
4. Call attention to the sentence on this handout: "Describe one person you know …" and give five minutes to complete the prompt.
5. Discuss responses.
6. Read aloud the Helen Keller quotation in the box at the bottom of the handout. Ask group members to identify which of the resilient characteristics are reflected in the quote.

VARIATIONS
1) Present five to ten characters in well-known books, movies, or newspaper clippings who portray characteristics of being resilient. Ask each group member to identify personal favorites.
2) At the end of each definition of the activity handout, ask group members to write the name of someone they know who represents that particular character trait of resiliency.
3) Ask each group member to identify one or more ways they do or can demonstrate resiliency.

NOTES

_____
_____
_____
_____
_____
_____
_____
_____
_____
_____

Topic VII — RESILIENCY

RESILIENCY: *Enjoy, Explore, & Experiment*

ENJOY!

What people do you enjoy?

_____
_____
_____
_____
_____
_____
_____

What do you enjoy?

_____
_____
_____
_____
_____
_____
_____

EXPLORE!

What have you experienced in the last month?
(Check the boxes and name the new experience.)

☐ New book _____
_____

☐ New place _____
_____

☐ New food _____
_____

☐ New friend _____
_____

☐ New hobby _____
_____

☐ New restaurant _____
_____

☐ New movie _____
_____

☐ Something other - new
_____

EXPERIMENT!

Make a discovery

About yourself:
_____
_____

About nature:
_____
_____
_____

About what you like to do:
_____
_____
_____

About what relaxes you:
_____
_____
_____

Other:
_____
_____
_____

Underline the words in this story that relate to ENJOYMENT, EXPLORATION, and/or EXPERIMENTATION.

I woke up this morning and wondered, **"What can I do today?"** I want to have fun and try something new and different. Maybe I can go to the bookstore? Maybe a movie? Try a new recipe? Get to that wonderful thrift shop? Maybe I can go to the zoo or park? Read poetry? Write poetry? Try journaling? Go to a counselor? Go to a coffee shop? Or I can spend the day in bed! Maybe I can rearrange things in the house to give it a different look? Spend time with people who help me feel really good about myself! **I have a lot of choices!**

> *Every morning when I wake up I say, "I'll never be as young as I am today. Today is the youngest day of the rest of my life. Get up and do something fun."*
>
> ~ Rochelle Ford, 78 year old metal sculptor

OPTIMAL WELL-BEING FOR SENIOR ADULTS II

RESILIENCY: *Enjoy, Explore, & Experiment*
Leader's Guide

PURPOSE
To pursue being actively engaged in three resilient characteristics: enjoying, experimenting, and exploring.

POSSIBLE NAMES OF SESSIONS
- *Enjoy … In Joy!*
- *The Three E's*
- *The Sunny Side of Life*

BACKGROUND INFORMATION
People who are resilient are actively engaged in several practices while enjoying, experimenting, and exploring. Examining them encourages an expansion and exchange of ideas. Personal reflection allows individuals to identify how to increase enjoyment, experimentation, and exploration in their own lives.

ACTIVITY
1. Explain to group that fostering resiliency is a daily practice.
2. Distribute handouts and pens.
3. Ask group members to complete the three vertical boxes.
4. After they are completed, discuss responses.
5. Read the story in the box slowly. Ask group to underline the words that relate to enjoyment, experimentation, and/or exploration.
6. Ask group members how they can foster these in their lives, using encouragement and problem solving.
7. Discuss quote at the bottom of the page.

VARIATIONS
For homework, encourage journaling on any or all of the words presented: enjoyment, experimentation, and exploration. In the next session, review journals for experiences and insights.

NOTES
_____
_____
_____
_____
_____
_____
_____
_____
_____
_____
_____
_____
_____
_____
_____
_____
_____

Topic VII — RESILIENCY

RESILIENCY: *Imagine, Innovate, & Invent*

A willingness to see something that isn't visible to ourselves and others is needed to imagine, innovate, and invent. For individuals or society to advance, these creative skills are extremely beneficial.

Imagine what life could look like in ten more years if a few of your life challenges were met.
_____
_____
_____

If you could invent a machine to help you, what would you invent?
_____
_____
_____

How could you simplify your life?
_____
_____
_____

Imagine either a perfect day, a perfect vacation, or a perfect meal.
_____
_____
_____

What is a creative gift that costs less than five dollars that you can give to a loved one?
_____
_____
_____

> *I said if he can do it, I'm gonna try.*
> ~ James Henry Arruda
> (Arruda taught himself to read at 92 years old and published a book at 96.)

OPTIMAL WELL-BEING FOR SENIOR ADULTS II

RESILIENCY: *Imagine, Innovate, & Invent*
Leader's Guide

PURPOSE
To pursue being actively engaged in three resiliency characteristics: imagining, innovating, and inventing.

POSSIBLE NAMES OF SESSIONS
- *The Three I's*
- *Crafting a New Future*
- *Expanding My Life*

BACKGROUND INFORMATION
People who are resilient are actively engaged in several practices, among them, imagining, innovating, and inventing. Examining and engaging in them encourages an expansion and exchange of ideas. Remind group members that throughout history, those who demonstrated these characteristics survived and helped humanity advance, e.g., Marie Curie, Jonas Salk, Bill Gates, and Dr. Temple Grandin. Although we might not aspire to be at the level of these individuals, we can certainly practice these three resiliency characteristics.

ACTIVITY
1. Explain to group that fostering resiliency is a daily practice.
2. Write the three words, imagine, innovate, and invent, on the board. Ask group members what famous people come to mind.
3. Distribute handouts and pens, explaining that we each have these characteristics and they need to be nurtured.
4. Give group members ten minutes to complete.
5. Share responses.
6. Facilitate ideas of how group members can use and foster these skills as a lifelong practice.

VARIATIONS
1) Discuss quote at the bottom of the page with the focus on relentless determination being a factor in imagining, innovating, and inventing.
2) Ask group members to identify someone who accomplished a goal they would like to pursue.

NOTES
_____
_____
_____
_____
_____
_____
_____
_____
_____
_____
_____
_____
_____
_____
_____

RESILIENCY: TAKE IT TO THE LIMIT

Today, what can I do to challenge myself in a good way?

PHYSICALLY

I can _____

_____
_____
_____
_____
_____

EMOTIONALLY

I can _____

_____
_____
_____
_____
_____

INTELLECTUALLY

I can _____

_____
_____
_____
_____
_____

RECREATIONALLY

I can _____

_____
_____
_____
_____
_____

INTERPERSONALLY

I can _____

_____
_____
_____
_____
_____

SPIRITUALLY

I can _____

_____
_____
_____
_____
_____

> You just don't let that rocking chair take over. You get up and go, even if you don't want to.
>
> ~ Constance Reeves, 102 year old cowgirl

OPTIMAL WELL-BEING FOR SENIOR ADULTS II

RESILIENCY: Take It to the Limit
Leader's Guide

PURPOSE
To pursue being actively engaged in fortifying resiliency by learning to take it to the limit.

POSSIBLE NAMES OF SESSIONS
- *Stretch Yourself*
- *Bringing Out My Very Best*
- *The Whole Me*

BACKGROUND INFORMATION
People who are resilient are actively engaged in several practices, and one is the activity to "take it to the limit," as long as it's reasonably safe. In this way, our capabilities expand and we become used to challenges in everyday life. *Today, what can I do to challenge myself in a good way?* is the question asked about six different aspects of everyday life.

ACTIVITY
1. Ask group members for examples of times in their lives when they were pleasantly surprised as they met a challenge.
2. Distribute handouts and pens.
3. Explain to group members that resilience is fostered in many ways towards taking challenges.
4. Give group members ten minutes to complete at least five of the six boxes.
5. Share results. Emphasize the results that accompany personal challenges: growth, self-confidence, bragging rights, willingness to take new challenges, fun, etc.

VARIATIONS
1) Offer group "Take it to the limit" journals in which individuals can document daily challenges.
2) Find group challenges that all participants can do:
   a. Physically – Stand on one foot for one minute.
   b. Emotionally – Talk about a difficult emotion, or read or write a prayer or blessing.
   c. Intellectually – Recall items on a tray after looking at them for only forty-five seconds.
   d. Recreationally – Watch a new musical or listen to a new song.
   e. Interpersonally – Pose an interesting question to a friend and really listen to the answer.

NOTES
_____
_____
_____
_____
_____
_____
_____
_____
_____
_____

Topic VII — RESILIENCY

RESILIENCY: Involve Self in the Greater Good

How can you be of service to others?
By giving time, energy, money, love, care, ideas, support, and what others most need.

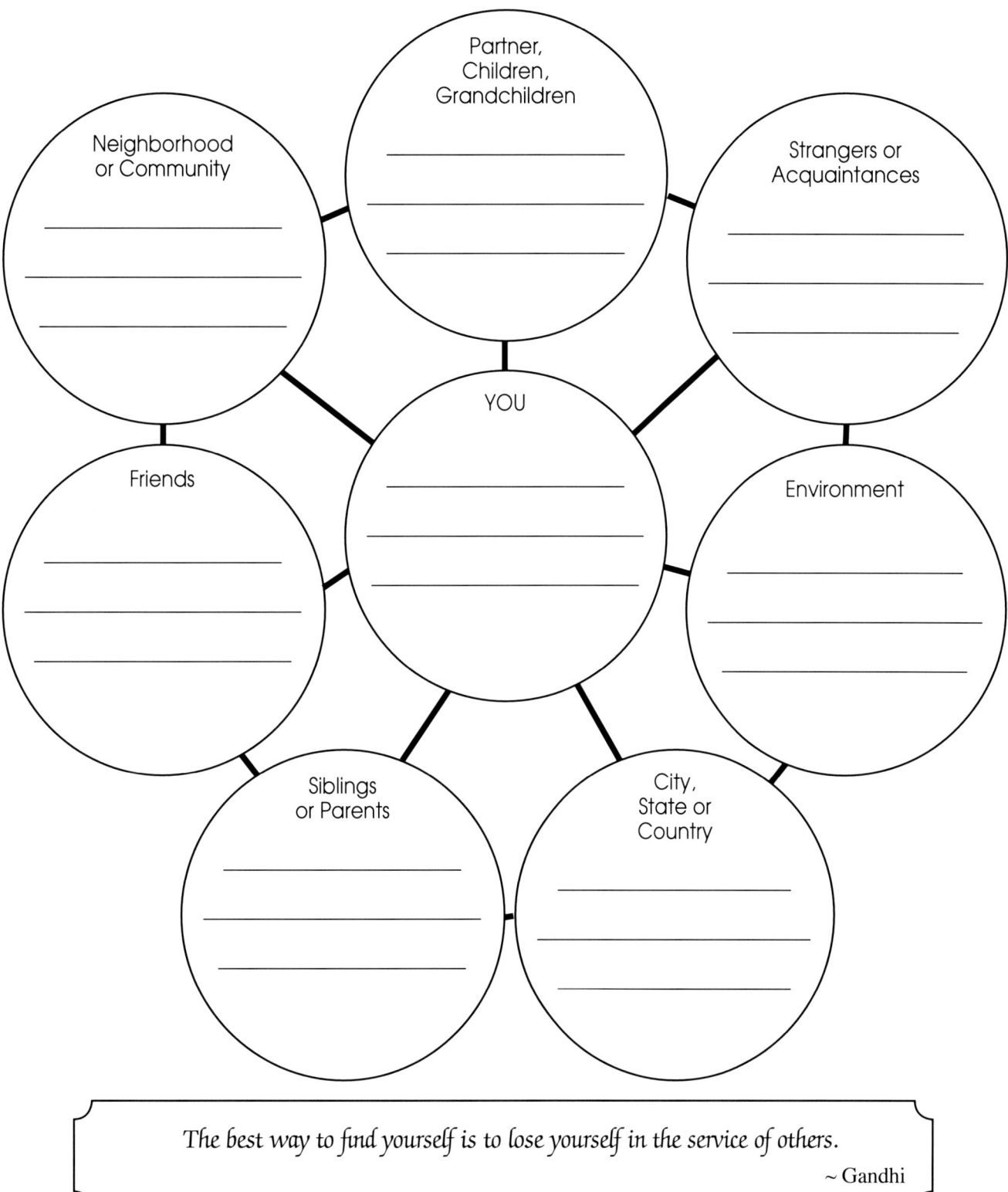

The best way to find yourself is to lose yourself in the service of others.
~ Gandhi

OPTIMAL WELL-BEING FOR SENIOR ADULTS II

RESILIENCY: Involve Self in the Greater Good
Leader's Guide

PURPOSE
To pursue being actively engaged in fortifying resiliency by involving oneself in the greater good.

POSSIBLE NAMES OF SESSIONS
- *Giving is a Beautiful Thing*
- *Altruism: Somebody Else*
- *Of Service to Others*

BACKGROUND INFORMATION
People who are resilient are actively engaged in several practices; among them is involving oneself in the greater good. Giving can include the gift of time, energy, money, love, ideas, support, material things, and other things people need. The question, "How can I be of service to others?" can be especially relevant to retired people who may be struggling with role identification and finding meaningful activities.

ACTIVITY
1. Read the quotation at the bottom of the page and discuss.
2. Expand on the concepts in background information.
3. Distribute handouts and pens.
4. Ask group members to complete five of the seven circles provided.
5. Discuss results asking group members to provide details of how they can be of service.
6. Emphasize the variety of ways that people can give.

VARIATIONS
Discuss positive childhood memories of adults giving of their time that had a positive impact on others. Emphasize the possibility of group members making a meaningful impact by serving others.

NOTES

Topic VIII
SAFETY
Table of Contents and Corresponding Goals for Each Section

At the end of the day, the goals are simple: safety and security.
~ Jodi Rell

Emergency Information 95
To be prepared by having important emergency information easily accessible.

Safety First 97
To increase safety awareness by evaluating responses to basic home safety questions.
To help determine level of independence and level of supervision needed to remain safe.

Kitchen Safety 99
To increase safety in the kitchen by reviewing basic safety guidelines.

Safe & Sound 101
To promote safety with senior adults.

Fact Sheet 103
To improve medication management by expanding knowledge of medications and the taking of those medications.

LEVEL OF UNDERSTANDING

 Basic Level    Intermediate Level    High Level

Topic VIII — SAFETY

Emergency Information

Place copies of this information in every room of the house and in your wallet and purse.

IF THERE IS AN EMERGENCY, CALL 9-1-1

My Emergency Contacts

Name _____ Phone Number(s) _____

Name _____ Phone Number(s) _____

Name _____ Phone Number(s) _____

Name _____ Phone Number(s) _____

Name _____ Phone Number(s) _____

Name _____ Phone Number(s) _____

My Primary Care Provider

Name _____ Phone Number(s) _____

Fold to the dashed line on top of the page

- -

Specialists

Specialty _____ Name _____ Phone Number(s) _____

Specialty _____ Name _____ Phone Number(s) _____

Specialty _____ Name _____ Phone Number(s) _____

Allergies _____

_____

_____

Notes *(pet care, spare key location, house access codes, etc.)* _____

_____

_____

_____

OPTIMAL WELL-BEING FOR SENIOR ADULTS II

Emergency Information
Leader's Guide

PURPOSE
To be prepared by having important emergency information easily accessible.

POSSIBLE NAMES OF SESSIONS
- *R U Ready?*
- *Cue Card*
- *Ready for an Emergency?*

BACKGROUND INFORMATION
Emergency situations generally cause confusion. Therefore, important emergency information located in strategic places can assist an individual during these stressful times. This cue card increases the probability of being able to keep the person who is at risk safe by effectively communicating with first responders. It may also help keep the home safe by allowing the first responders to call the emergency contacts.

ACTIVITY
1. Distribute the handouts and explain the purpose of the Emergency Information cue card.
2. Ask each individual to complete. Use telephone books or computer search engines, if necessary.
3. Ask individuals what other information that they would like to see on this card. Encourage them to write it in the section at the bottom marked **"Notes."**
4. Photocopy as many for each individual as needed on color paper/card stock.
5. Instruct group members to fold the sheet from one dashed line to the other, to ensure privacy if posting in a location visible to others.
6. Role play emergency situations with cue card to ensure that all details are properly considered if an emergency occurs.

VARIATIONS
Use with a client who is being discharged from a facility along with family members.

NOTES
_____
_____
_____
_____
_____
_____
_____
_____
_____
_____
_____
_____
_____
_____
_____

Topic VIII — SAFETY

Safety First

In each box, answer the following questions to check your safety awareness.

1. Do you have throw rugs or other obstacles on your floor?

2. How do you get something off of a high shelf?

3. Why are nightlights in many places helpful and important?

4. Do you have smoke detectors in your place of living?
   How many?
   How often should you check them?

5. What would you wear if you were going to be outside for 10 minutes or more and the temperture is below freezing?

6. What would you do if you smelled gas in your home?

7. Do you have an electrical cord running across any of your floors or pathways?
   What might be the problem with that?

8. Is it ever okay for you, or anyone else, to smoke in bed?
   Why or why not?

9. Do you have a cell phone with you at all times, or do you have a telephone in every room?

10. What type of bath mat is a good idea?

What are your safety concerns? _____

_____

_____

_____

_____

_____

OPTIMAL WELL-BEING FOR SENIOR ADULTS II

Safety First
Leader's Guide

PURPOSE
To increase safety awareness by evaluating responses to basic home safety questions. To help determine level of independence and level of supervision needed to remain safe.

POSSIBLE NAMES OF SESSIONS
- *I Want to Be Safe!*
- *Safety is a Serious Matter*
- *What to Do to Keep Safe*

BACKGROUND INFORMATION
Safety is a major concern of everyone involved with senior adults. Fires and falls are just a few of the concerns. Answering questions about safety will serve as a screening to help determine how safe an individual is, and how much assistance might be needed. Further assessment would be needed if red flags of unsafe behavior were detected. Answers to questions can also be used to gain information about cognitive functioning skills such as problem solving, decision-making, reality orientation and judgement. Insight can also be observed.

ACTIVITY
1. Distribute handouts and pens.
2. Ask group members to complete the handout or discuss each question and response.
3. As a group, discuss all responses and facilitate feedback from group members. NOTE: Not all questions may be appropriate for all participants. Use discretion and ask for clarification whenever a group member's responses are unclear.
4. Review last question, delving into personal safety concerns.
5. Process benefits of safety in the home and the risks of not being safe.

VARIATIONS
1) Handout index cards. Ask group members to write a 'safety scenario' on their cards. For example, "You are home alone and you hear noises outside of your window. What is the best thing to do?" Switch index cards with a partner. Have group members read each other's questions and respond. Reconvene as a large group and share results of the exercise.
2) Create additional questions or use the following:
   a. What should you do if there is a tornado warning?
   b. How can you tell when chicken is thoroughly cooked?
   c. Whom should you call if you lose power or water in your home?
   d. Whom would you call if you needed a ride to an appointment?
   e. When should you lock your doors?
3) Create additional questions focusing on health issues:
   a. What would you do if you were having chest pains?
   b. Whom do you call if you have severe flu symptoms? Do you know the telephone number? If yes, what is it?
   c. Where would you go to have your blood pressure checked?

NOTES
___
___
___
___
___
___
___
___

Kitchen Safety

Check (✓) if yes. In your kitchen, do you currently have ...

☐ a fire extinguisher?
☐ a chair close by to rest if needed?
☐ a strong and balanced step stool close by if needed to reach items from a high place?
☐ electrical appliances in good repair?
☐ a non-skid mat?
☐ pot holders?
☐ anti-bacterial soap for hands?
☐ other? _____
☐ other? _____
☐ other? _____

Rate Your Safety Practices by putting the correct number in the boxes.

NEVER DO	HARDLY EVER	SOMETIMES	USUALLY	ALWAYS
1	2	3	4	5

Do you ...

☐ turn the stove off after cooking?
☐ make sure the kitchen floor is free from clutter?
☐ store knives in wooden block or drawer?
☐ make sure the kitchen floor is dry before walking on it?
☐ turn pot handles away from front of stove?
☐ put temperature-sensitive foods in refrigerator or freezer in a timely fashion?
☐ wash vegetables and fruit before eating them?
☐ know the number of days food can be refrigerated before it needs to be discarded.

Kitchen Safety
Leader's Guide

PURPOSE
To increase safety in the kitchen by reviewing basic safety guidelines.

POSSIBLE NAMES OF SESSIONS
- *Kitchen Safety Reminders*
- *Kitchen Cues*
- *Better Safe Than Sorry*

BACKGROUND INFORMATION
Kitchens are a frequent place for falls, burns, cuts, and accidental fires. It can be helpful to objectively look at kitchen safety when not in the kitchen itself. Food handling and storage safety are equally important.

ACTIVITY
1. Introduce and explain purpose of the checklist.
2. Distribute handouts and pens for notes.
3. Discuss the items in the checklist and the relevance of each item, and ask group members to complete their lists at the same time.
4. Assist group members in setting goals to increase kitchen safety.

VARIATIONS
1) Demonstrate helpful kitchen equipment that might promote safety. *(Example: kitchen timer, oven mitts, one-handed adaptive tools, fire extinguisher, etc.)*
2) Demonstrate or show pictures of injury-prone areas in the kitchen. *(Example: floor rugs, frayed cords, telephone lines on floor, towels by the stove, water or food on the floor.)* Discuss how to prevent accidents or injuries in the kitchen.

NOTES

Topic VIII — SAFETY

Safe & Sound

Check carefully to avoid potential safety problems.

Answer these questions honestly with a ✔ in the yes or no column.
Respond as if someone were to walk in your living space right now.

#	Questions	Yes	No
1	Do you have all loose floor rugs secured with non-slip mats under them?		
2	Are all pieces of furniture sturdy and balanced so they do not wobble?		
3	If needed, do you have adaptive equipment in the bathroom? *Example: grab bars, raised toilet seat, non-slip bath mat or rug.*		
4	Do you have a list of easy-to-read emergency phone numbers? *Example: doctors' names, family members' phone numbers.*		
5	Do you have properly working smoke detectors?		
6	Do you have a working, up-to-date, fire extinguisher in the kitchen?		
7	When you are home, do you always wear sensible, well-fitting shoes and/or slippers?		
8	Are tight spots clutter-free?		
9	Are stairways clutter-free?		
10	Do you have adequate lighting for walking at night to the bathroom and/or the kitchen?		
11	Are commonly used items in the bathroom reachable without a step stool?		
12	Are commonly used items in the kitchen reachable without a step stool?		
13	Do you have a telephone in every room or do you keep your cell phone with you at all times?		

Consider that any NOs
may indicate that you need to adapt your environment to prevent an accident or injury.

OPTIMAL WELL-BEING FOR SENIOR ADULTS II

Safe & Sound
Leader's Guide

PURPOSE
To promote safety with senior adults.

POSSIBLE NAMES OF SESSIONS
- *Safety First*
- *Preventing Accidents at Home … Today!*
- *Is Your Living Space Safe?*

BACKGROUND INFORMATION
Falls and fires are just a few of the safety hazards with the senior adult population. Adapting the environment may require a little thought, time, and money, but could prevent a serious accident and keep someone at home … safe and sound!

ACTIVITY
1. Distribute handouts and pens.
2. Give group members ten minutes to complete handouts. Emphasize honesty.
3. Discuss each item. Problem solve ways to increase safety when participants indicate "no."
4. Bring adaptive equipment, lighting, and other household equipment catalogues (with fire extinguisher, non-slip pads, lighting) to review availability and costs of needed products. Review and discuss.
5. Explain that the costs spent on preventing an accident would be substantially less than if an accident actually occurred.

VARIATIONS
1) Bring adaptive equipment to group session and demonstrate its usefulness. Display an attitude of "You might not need this today, but please consider that someday these might be helpful, and it's good to know about them."
2) Before the group session, show either hand-drawn pictures, computer print-outs, photos, or cutouts from magazines of potential hazards (example: wet floors, dangling or frayed cords, unsafe electrical outlets, etc.) in the home and discuss.
3) Ask group members to create "Safety First" posters or flyers.

NOTES
_____
_____
_____
_____
_____
_____
_____
_____
_____
_____
_____
_____

Topic VIII — SAFETY

Fact Sheet

Everything you always wanted to know about medications.

FACTS ABOUT OVER THE COUNTER MEDICATIONS (OTC)

1. Non-prescription medications are intended to relieve symptoms of minor ailments. If conditions persist, see your doctor.
2. Some over-the-counter medications should NOT be taken with other medications. They may interfere with their effectiveness or have harmful effects. Check with your pharmacist if you are unsure.
3. There is information on the labels that warns people who have special health problems.
4. If in doubt about purchasing an OTC medication, ask your pharmacist. This can help prevent medical issues.

THE NEVER'S ABOUT MEDICATIONS

1. Never discontinue medications on your own.
2. Never take someone else's medications.
3. Never give your medication to someone else.
4. Never take the labels off of your medication containers.
5. Never leave medications within the reach of children.
6. Never combine different medications in the same bottle.
7. Never take a new medication without checking with a doctor or pharmacist to be sure it's compatible with your other medications.
8. Never go far from home without a list of medications.

DID YOU KNOW?

1. Store all of your medications in a cool, dry place. This most likely is NOT your bathroom medicine cabinet!
2. Some medications may cause drowsiness, can make it dangerous to operate a car, or make you susceptible to falls.
3. Some medicine bottles come with easy-to-open caps. Request it from your pharmacist.
4. Different medications take different lengths of time to have a noticeable effect.
5. Prescription medication for mental illnesses do not take the place of therapy or counseling.
6. It may take some time for a doctor to find the right medication and dose for you. Every person is affected differently by medications. Be patient! Don't give up!
7. You should not drive when taking certain medications.
8. It is best to get all of your medications from one pharmacy.
9. You can request updated lists of your medications from your pharmacy.

OPTIMAL WELL-BEING FOR SENIOR ADULTS II

Fact Sheet
Leader's Guide

PURPOSE
To improve medication management by expanding knowledge of medications and the taking of those medications.

POSSIBLE NAMES OF SESSIONS
- *What You Need to Know About Meds*
- *Just the Facts*
- *Medications – Knowledge Applied is Power*

BACKGROUND INFORMATION
Medication management can be a difficult task but is vital for many people to control symptoms. Once symptoms are controlled, other functional performance areas oftentimes fall into place. It is wise to include supportive family/friends/partners in the medication management process.

ACTIVITY
1. Distribute handouts and pens.
2. Review the material, encouraging brief discussion for each item covered.
3. Facilitate a fifteen-minute question and answer period.
4. Add to the "Did You Know" list with group input and/or with items such as …
   a. Dizziness may occur with some medications. If this is the case, change positions slowly.
   b. Each doctor needs to be aware of every medication a patient takes.
5. Process the session, using the *Knowledge is Power* concept.
6. Display weekly medication containers and encourage group members to set up their morning, afternoon, evening, and bedtime doses. Provide assistance if needed.

VARIATIONS
1) Invite a pharmacist to speak to the group about medications.
2) Role-play with group members possible situations.
   a. A trip to the doctor's office.
   b. An interaction with someone urging the person to discontinue his/her medications.
   c. An interaction with a supportive person dealing with this issue: "But I don't want to take medications my whole life."

NOTES

Topic IX
MINDFULNESS
Table of Contents and Corresponding Goals for Each Section

Mindfulness is about being fully awake in our lives. It is about perceiving the exquisite vividness of each moment. We also gain immediate access to our own powerful inner resources for insight, transformation, and healing.

~ Jon Kabat-Zinn

Mindfulness vs. Busy Mind 107
To understand basic characteristics of mindfulness vs. a busy mind.

Exploring My Journey 109
To explore the spiritual journey with words, metaphors, and images.

Spiritual Themes 111
To gain awareness of the variety of spiritual themes that operate in everyday life.
To foster spiritual themes that are in one's life.

Weathering Spiritual Seasons 113
To explore and accept a variety of spiritual feelings and experiences.

Mindful Practices 115
To cultivate mindful practices.

LEVEL OF UNDERSTANDING

 Basic Level    Intermediate Level    High Level

Topic IX — MINDFULNESS

Mindfulness vs. Busy Mind

MINDFULNESS	VS.	BUSY MIND
Focus on breath		Caught up in thoughts and feelings
Observes; notices		Reacts
Focus on bodily sensations		Distracted
Focus on here and now		Dwelling on past or future
Awareness		Uninformed - clueless
Distancing from thoughts and feelings		Holding onto thoughts and feelings
Ability to gently bring mind back		Mind running away with repetitive or unrelated thoughts and feelings
Peaceful; quiet; relaxed; tranquil		Easily frustrated
Grounded		Judgmental
Centered		Critical of self and others
Grateful		Feelings of lacking or missing out
Clarity		Fogginess
More positivity; less negativity		More negativity; less positivity

My personal reflections on mindfulness vs. busy mind.

_____

_____

_____

Mindfulness vs. Busy Mind
Leader's Guide

PURPOSE
To understand basic characteristics of mindfulness vs. a busy mind.

POSSIBLE NAMES OF SESSIONS
- *What is Mindfulness?*
- *Busy Mind, Busy Body*
- *Mindful or Mind Full*

BACKGROUND INFORMATION
Mindfulness is frequently mentioned in popular culture. This activity explores the characteristics of both mindfulness and the busy mind. Through this exploration, mindfulness will develop into a desirable pursuit.

ACTIVITY
1. To determine prior knowledge, ask group members what they know about mindfulness.
2. Distribute handouts and pens.
3. Discuss point-by-point, allowing group members to elaborate, and use personal examples or anecdotes.
4. Introduce a simple breathing exercise for two or three minutes. Guide group members to sit in a supported position, and gently direct the focus on the breath vs. thoughts.
5. Process the breathing exercise.
6. Process the benefits group members see for themselves through mindfulness.

VARIATIONS
From books or the internet, find guided imagery scripts that focus on mindfulness. Encourage the group to choose one or two for a follow-up session.

NOTES

Topic IX — MINDFULNESS

Exploring My Journey

Each of us has a unique journey

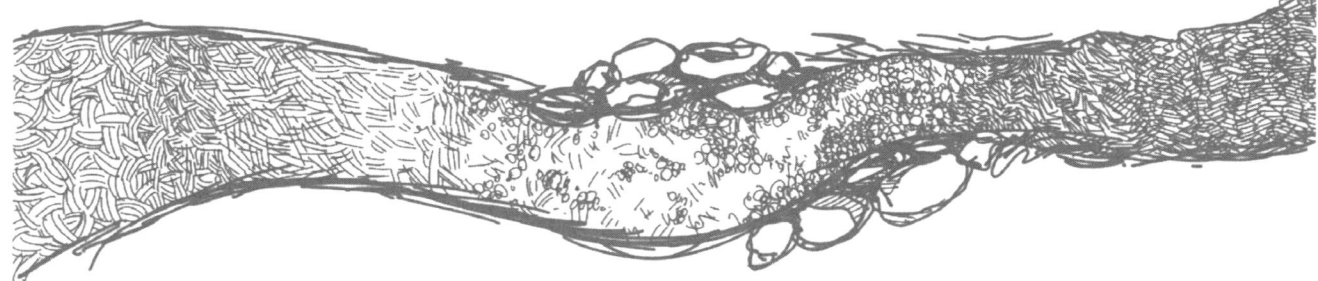

One way to honor our unique journey is to look at it with words, metaphors, and images. Respond to the following:

1. **Listed below are two phrases. Which one could you adopt as a daily reminder to be mindful and present?** *(Check one and/or add another.)*
   ___ A. Be here now
   ___ B. This too shall pass
   ___ C. Other phrase _____

2. **If I slow down, I can** _____
   _____

3. **Which are you most like?** *(Check one)*
   ___ A. Flowing stream
   ___ B. Large rushing waterfall
   ___ C. Tranquil lake

4. **If I could get clarity about** _____
   _____ my quality of life would most likely improve.

5. **Which animal most represents who or what you are like?** *(Check one)*
   ___ A. Bull   ___ B. Dog   ___ C. Eagle   ___ D. Pack rat   ___ E. Rabbit

   Explain your choice: _____

6. **Ways I am more likely to pursue my spiritual path with or through:** *(Check all that apply)*

   ___ A. Alone
   ___ B. Books
   ___ C. Music
   ___ D. Nature
   ___ E. Religious or Spiritual Community
   ___ F. Other People
   ___ G. Poetry
   ___ H. Spiritual Leader or Clergy
   ___ I. Yoga
   ___ J. Other

OPTIMAL WELL-BEING FOR SENIOR ADULTS II

Exploring My Journey
Leader's Guide

PURPOSE
To explore the spiritual journey with words, metaphors, and images.

POSSIBLE NAMES OF SESSIONS
- *My Unique Journey*
- *Seeing My Path Clearly*
- *The Road to My Spirituality*

BACKGROUND INFORMATION
Many people might not relate to the term spiritual journey, but could easily relate to specific questions about a *unique journey*. Opportunities to explore a spiritual journey in a safe, accepting environment may provide a deeper understanding of the jewels that are typically found during the journey.

ACTIVITY
1. Draw a windy path on the board.
2. Explain that a person's journey in life is typically more like a winding path vs. a straight highway. It takes both community and courage to explore one's personal journey; however, it may reap rewards.
3. Distribute handouts and pens.
4. Play soft music while group members complete the handout.
5. Divide group members into pairs and offer several minutes for individuals to interview each other.
6. Focus on question number six on the handout, offering support and encouragement.

VARIATIONS
To further journey exploration, bring all types of books or a list of categories that may interest individuals in the group.

NOTES

Topic IX — MINDFULNESS

Spiritual Themes

Spiritual themes are often apparent in mindful or conscious living.

Match the spiritual theme on the left with its definition on the right.

1. Hope	A. Quality of being kind and giving. _____
2. Compassion	B. Intense feelings of affection. _____
3. Gratitude	C. Concern for suffering of others. _____
4. Forgiveness	D. Feelings of great pleasure and happiness. _____
5. Generosity	E. Feelings of expectation and desire for a certain thing to happen. _____
6. Empathy	F. Ability to identify with, or understand and share, another's experiences and feelings. _____
7. Faith	G. Decision to release feelings of resentment towards another. _____
8. Love	H. Based in reality; with fact; actuality. _____
9. Peace	I. Plain; natural; easy to understand. _____
10. Truth	J. Freedom from disturbance. _____
11. Joy	K. Act of taking what is offered. _____
12. Simplicity	L. Complete trust in someone or something. _____
13. Acceptance	M. Quality of being thankful. _____

OPTIMAL WELL-BEING FOR SENIOR ADULTS II

Spiritual Themes
Leader's Guide

PURPOSE

To gain awareness of the variety of spiritual themes that operate in everyday life.

To foster spiritual themes that are in one's life.

POSSIBLE NAMES OF SESSIONS

- *Spiritual Themes*
- *What do I Value Most?*
- *Definitions of Spiritual Themes*

BACKGROUND INFORMATION

Spiritual themes are not dependent on religious practices. They can be fostered through words and actions. Defining them will provide an avenue for ensuring a common understanding for group members.

ACTIVITY

1. Introduce the topic using background information.
2. List a few of the spiritual themes on the board and ask group members to share ideas about definitions.
3. Distribute pens or pencils.
4. Present handouts and divide group into pairs.
5. Ask pairs to complete handouts within ten minutes.
6. Reconvene group members. Ask individuals to star the "Top 3" that they would most like to experience more in their lives.
7. Problem solve as a group to define practical ways to do this.

VARIATIONS

Ask the group how they feel about the Law of Attraction. (If they are unfamiliar with the phrase, explain: *The law of attraction is the name given to the maxim "like attracts like" which is used to sum up the idea that by focusing on positive or negative thoughts people bring positive or negative experiences into their lives.*)

Do group members believe that if they demonstrate spiritual themes, they will attract them in their lives?

ANSWER KEY		
A – 5	F – 6	K – 13
B – 8	G – 4	L – 7
C – 2	H – 10	M – 3
D – 11	I – 12	
E – 1	J – 9	

NOTES

_____
_____
_____
_____
_____
_____
_____
_____
_____
_____

Topic IX — MINDFULNESS

WEATHERING SPIRITUAL SEASONS

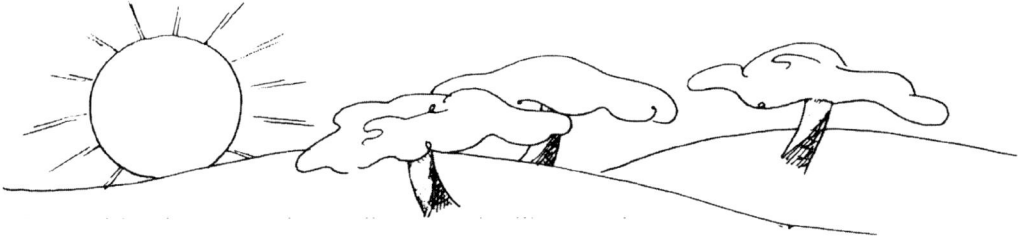

**The spiritual patterns of our lives can be like weather patterns or 'seasons.'
The spiritual quest is how you EXPERIENCE these patterns or 'seasons.'**

1. Describe in detail your current spiritual pattern using weather terms, if appropriate. *(autumn, drought, fierce storm, freezing cold, hurricane, pelting hail, relentless heat, spring-time, teeming sleet, summer, sunny, tornado, torrents of rain, winter, etc.)*

   _____
   _____
   _____
   _____
   _____
   _____

2. What feelings or thoughts accompany this season?

   _____
   _____
   _____
   _____
   _____
   _____

3. Explore some sources of spiritual light that accompany you.

   _____
   _____
   _____
   _____
   _____
   _____

Weathering Spiritual Seasons
Leader's Guide

PURPOSE
To explore and accept a variety of spiritual feelings and experiences.

POSSIBLE NAMES OF SESSIONS
- *Let it Shine*
- *The Weather Outside is Frightful, But …*
- *What Does it Take to Weather a Storm?*

BACKGROUND INFORMATION
It is not unusual for people recovering from a trauma or illness, or who are experiencing the challenges that come with aging, to buy into magical thinking and pursue the "ideal" religious experience. This can lead to disappointment, discouragement, and perhaps abandonment of this important part of our life experience. Exposing participants to a variety of *spiritual* 'seasons' may help normalize the highs and lows of those spiritual experiences.

ACTIVITY
1. Explain that our spiritual attitudes and lives are often related.
2. Distribute handouts and pens.
3. Read each section together as a group. Allow group members a few minutes to complete the lines.
4. Discuss and provide supportive atmosphere for sharing. See if there are any similarities re: seasons or experiences.
5. Make a large list of all responses for spiritual 'light' on the board, with no repeats.
6. Discuss the possibilities available to bring the 'light' into our lives.

VARIATIONS
1) Introduce the concept of drawing a 'seasonal vignette.' This drawing should reflect how one is feeling, using a nature theme that will reflect the artist's spirit. Have a variety of art media available.
2) Discuss how photographs can capture a sense of spirit. Collect photos and show them to the group one by one. Ask group members to reflect on how each photo relates to spiritual seasons.

NOTES

Topic IX — MINDFULNESS

Mindful Practices

*Mindfulness means paying attention in a particular way –
with intention, in the present, and in an accepting manner.*

Most people agree that mindful and conscious living is a healthier choice than living life lacking awareness and clarity. But how to achieve this is highly individual and personal. This handout provides a variety of practices for you to reflect upon and consider.

PRACTICE	MY EXPERIENCE WITH IT …	HOW I CAN SUPPORT MYSELF IF I WANT TO PURSUE AND DEEPEN MY PRACTICES.
Conscious Eating		
Conscious Drinking		
Meditation		
Mindful Walking		
Yoga		
Dream Exploration		
Journaling		
Mindful Breathing		
Slowing Down		
Other _____		
Other _____		
Other _____		
Other _____		

OPTIMAL WELL-BEING FOR SENIOR ADULTS II

Mindful Practices
Leader's Guide

PURPOSE

To cultivate mindful practices.

POSSIBLE NAMES OF SESSIONS

- *Practicing Mindfully*
- *Practice, Practice, Practice*
- *Cultivating Mindful Practices*

BACKGROUND INFORMATION

Mindfulness does not conflict with any beliefs, religions, or cultural traditions. It offers a way of being in the world with awareness, clarity, and acceptance. This handout will serve as an introduction or survey of possible practices.

ACTIVITY

1. Distribute handouts and pens.
2. Read top paragraph to group members.
3. Proceed with each practice by exploring prior or current experience, and ways to support or pursue the practices.
4. Provide resources (city, county, state, or national websites; names of experts in the field) to cultivate practices.
5. Close group with conscious eating of raisins, examining color, size, texture, and taste with awareness.

VARIATIONS

Discuss potential benefits of mindfulness: less reactivity, less judgement; fewer severe physical symptoms; and greater energy and enthusiasm for life.

NOTES

_____
_____
_____
_____
_____
_____
_____
_____
_____
_____
_____
_____
_____
_____
_____
_____
_____

Topic X

THINKING SKILLS
Table of Contents and Corresponding Goals for Each Section

Problems are not the problem; coping is the problem.
~ Virginia Satir

Steps to a Healthy Brain 119
To introduce basic concepts for good brain health.

Crossword Puzzle 121
To use problem solving skills to increase awareness of commonly used terms in mental health and aging programs.

KEEP ON THINKING 123
To challenge logical and abstract thinking in a fun and supportive environment.

S-T-R-E-T-C-H Your Mind 125
To engage in creative, brain boosting activities.

Haiku Fun 127
To challenge creative thinking skills by composing haikus.

LEVEL OF UNDERSTANDING

 Basic Level    Intermediate Level    High Level

Topic X — THINKING SKILLS

STEPS to a Healthy Brain

NOTES _____
_____
_____
_____
_____
_____
_____
_____
_____
_____
_____
_____
_____

Choose healthy fats	
Drink green tea	
Drink plenty of water	
Eat dairy foods for calcium	
Eat leafy greens	
Eat nuts	
Enjoy fish	
Eat lots of protein	
Eat whole grain carbs	
Follow doctor's orders for special diet needs	
Increase fresh fruit intake	
Maintain proper weight	
Read labels	
Reduce caffeine	
Reduce sugar	

Engage in regular physical activity

Exercise

Maintain proper weight

Stay active

Take short naps

Respect amount of sleep that works for you

Stay fit

Maintain good posture

Keep a positive attitude

No smoking

Low alcohol intake

No illegal substances

No tobacco

1. **Test your recall:** *What did you eat for breakfast? What color is your underwear?*
2. **Learn something new.** *New card game. A few words from a language you don't know. Email Social media*
3. **Try a new recipe.** *A healthy salad with home grown herbs.*
4. **Do math without paper, pen, or calculator.** *Work on your checking account or credit card bill.*
5. **Challenge your hand-eye coordination.** *Play catch. Juggle. Play ping pong.*
6. **Draw what you feel & what you remember.** *A map of your city. A floor plan from your previous home.*
7. **Play games or do puzzles - old familiar ones and new ones.** *Monopoly Bridge Crossword puzzles*

OPTIMAL WELL-BEING FOR SENIOR ADULTS II

sTEPS to a Healthy Brain
Leader's Guide

PURPOSE
Introduce basic concepts for good brain health.

POSSIBLE NAMES OF SESSIONS
- *Good Brain Health*
- *Ways to Boost Brain Power*
- *Stepping Up My Brain Power*

BACKGROUND INFORMATION
It is important for seniors to be educated about what they can do to optimize brain health. The holistic approach presented in this handout provides information about diet, exercise, alcohol, drugs, and activities.

ACTIVITY
1. Review with group members that the brain is the main organ of the nervous system and the command center. It records, processes, utilizes, stores, and retrieves vast quantities of information at the "speed of thought."
2. Distribute handouts and pens.
3. Discuss step-by-step the steps to a healthy brain, beginning with the first step on the left, and conclude with the largest step on the right.
4. Encourage problem-solving and note-taking by engaging group members in creative activities that they can easily participate in nourishing a healthy brain.

VARIATIONS
1) Invite a nutritionist to discuss current brain research and how it relates to nutrition.
2) Invite a personal trainer to discuss possible exercise programs to achieve regular physical activity.
3) Bring examples of crossword puzzles and other games. Encourage group members to explore their cell phones or computers for brain boosting games.

NOTES
_____
_____
_____
_____
_____
_____
_____
_____
_____
_____
_____
_____

Crossword Puzzle

Topic X — THINKING SKILLS

Here are clues to some aging and/or mental health terms:

ACROSS

2. A professional who listens and works toward mental wellness
4. A theme that might appear in a senior adult's life that needs to be resolved – but not necessarily forgotten
6. Abbreviation for over the counter drugs
7. Feeling separated from others and alone
8. What needs to be exercised in senior adulthood? Sometimes associated with the common expression "use it or lose it"
11. Often nervous, tense, high-strung, worried
12. Persistent sadness over time

DOWN

1. What some people do to relieve symptoms; not a recommended course of action.
3. Friends, family, or agencies who help you and care about you and advocate for your best interest
5. A term that includes a variety of disorders including anxiety, depression, bipolar, schizophrenia, and personality disorders
9. The natural process that begins the moment we are born and continues over the years
10. What we leave for generations to come

Crossword Puzzle
Leader's Guide

PURPOSE
To use problem solving skills to increase awareness of commonly used terms in mental health and aging programs.

POSSIBLE NAMES OF SESSIONS
- *Crossword Puzzle with a Mission*
- *Oh, I Get It!*
- *Do You Have a Clue?*

BACKGROUND INFORMATION
Terms are often used without everyone's understanding. Some people are shy or embarrassed and don't ask for an explanation while others may understand terms. A review of the meanings of commonly used terms in a fun, non-threatening way will literally put everyone on the same page.

Hyphenated words have no hyphen or space between them.

A two-word phrase has no space between the two words.

ACTIVITY
1. Distribute handouts and pens.
2. Review purpose of this crossword puzzle.
3. Divide group in pairs or allow group members to do the puzzle individually, depending on their skill level and interest.
4. Give group ten to fifteen minutes to complete.
5. Review answers and allow group members to discuss terms. Provide information not found in clues.
6. Ask group members to make an additional list of commonly heard terms used by professionals, other people, or in the literature.

VARIATIONS
1) Develop a word search of terms listed in Activity #6.
2) Tally group members to see which of the terms need further exploration.

ANSWER TO CLUES KEY

Across
2. THERAPIST
4. FORGIVENESS
6. OTC
7. ISOLATED
8. BRAIN
11. ANXIOUS
12. DEPRESSION

Down
1. SELF-MEDICATE
3. SUPPORTS
5. MENTAL ILLNESS
9. AGING
10. LEGACY

NOTES
_____
_____
_____
_____
_____
_____
_____
_____
_____
_____

Topic X — THINKING SKILLS

KEEP ON THINKING

1. In 60 seconds, write all the words that you can think of that begin with the letter "S."
   No proper nouns. No numbers. No names.
   Do not use the same word with different suffixes (sit, sitting, sitter).

   _____
   _____
   _____
   _____
   _____
   _____

2. Write your ideas about the following sayings:

   Don't cry over spilled milk. _____
   _____

   A penny saved is a penny earned _____
   _____

   Actions speak louder than words. _____
   _____

3. What did you eat for your last meal? Write as many details as you can remember _____
   _____
   _____
   _____
   _____
   _____
   _____

4. BONUS: What does this encrypted message say?

   25 15 21   3 18 1 3 11 5 4   20 8 5   3 15 4 5 !
   __ __ __   __ __ __ __ __ __ __   __ __ __   __ __ __ __ !

OPTIMAL WELL-BEING FOR SENIOR ADULTS II

KEEP ON THINKING
Leader's Guide

PURPOSE
To challenge logical and abstract thinking in a fun and supportive environment.

POSSIBLE NAMES OF SESSIONS
- *Boost Brain Power*
- *Brain Food*
- *I Think I Can, I Think I Can*

BACKGROUND INFORMATION
Use it or lose it is a philosophy for maintaining skills and abilities. This applies to cognitive skills as well. This handout provides a variety of skill challenges.

ACTIVITY
1. Explain the concepts in the Background Information above.
2. Distribute handouts and pens.
3. Complete each section with group members using answers below for explanation and discussions.
4. Encourage all group members to foster good "thinking" skills in every possible way.

VARIATIONS
1) Introduce distractions such as music to increase difficulty.
2) Show a variety of books, workbooks, internet sites with similar challenges.

ANSWERS
1. Review need for quick thinking: Generating specific thoughts in a time limited capacity is a great life skill.
   (0-5 = fair; 6-10 – just above fair; 11+ = good.)
2. Review the need for abstract thinking.
   Don't cry over spilled milk. It doesn't help to be upset over past events.
   A penny saved is a penny earned. Money not spent is money you have.
   Actions speak louder than words. What someone does is more important than what someone says.
3. Review need for mindfulness and memory: Eating can be a great mindfulness practice and easy to recall when doing so.
4. Review need to take in difficult challenges for boosted brain power.
   A = 1 …. Z = 26
   YOU CRACKED THE CODE!

NOTES
_____
_____
_____
_____
_____
_____
_____
_____

Topic X — THINKING SKILLS

S-T-R-E-T-C-H Your Mind

**You exercise your brain by doing or learning new and different things.
Creativity can stretch your mind.
Here are three different types of stretching your mind. Have FUN!**

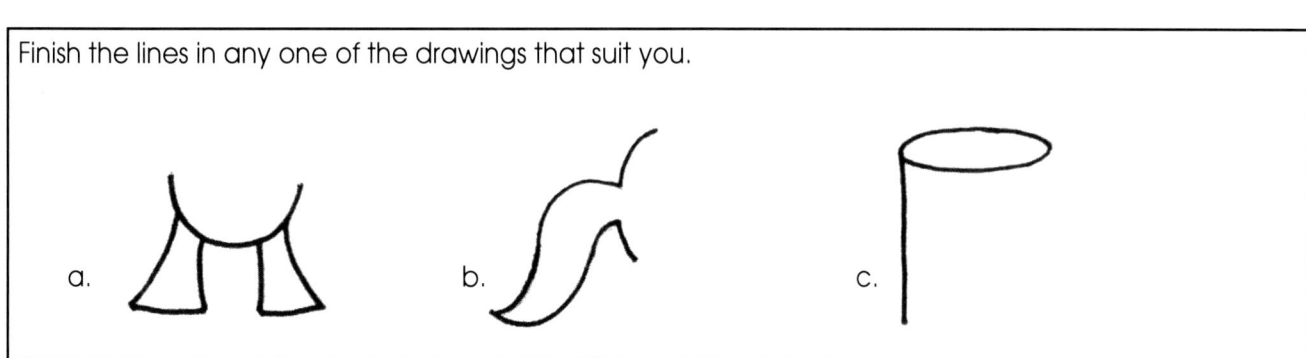

I. What would you eat if you were granted one entire meal low in calories with no fat and sugar?

II. If you could invent a machine that would make your day easier or more pleasant, what would it do?

What would you call it?

S-T-R-E-T-C-H Your Mind
Leader's Guide

PURPOSE
To engage in creative, brain-boosting activities.

POSSIBLE NAMES OF SESSIONS
- *Creative Thinking*
- *Thinking Outside of the Box*
- *I Can Do It.*

BACKGROUND INFORMATION
These creative brain-boosting activities are success oriented because they don't have right or wrong answers. They can be playful and interesting, and they offer a new view of an individual.

ACTIVITY
1. Distribute handouts and pens.
2. Emphasize that there are no right or wrong answers.
3. Instruct group members to do the first section. Offer an example on the flipchart if needed. Discuss responses. Support creativity and unique responses.
4. Now, instruct group members to do the second section. Offer an example on the flipchart if needed. Discuss responses. Support creativity and unique responses.
5. Next, instruct group members to answer the questions in the third section. Discuss the responses in an atmosphere of creativity and discovery.

VARIATIONS
1) Develop a list of creative questions or use these for more fun in a follow-up group, if time allows.
   a. If you were granted one wish that you could be sure would last for one hundred years, what would it be?
   b. If you could be responsible for one memorable 'first,' what would it be?
      I'd be the first person to _____
   c. Collect one favorite response from each person, cut and paste to create a poster titled OUR FAVORITES. Hang the poster in a place chosen by group members.
2) Find creative puzzle, optical illusion, and quiz books from a local bookstore or library, and share!

NOTES
_____
_____
_____
_____
_____
_____
_____
_____
_____

Topic X — THINKING SKILLS

Haiku Fun

**Haikus are a Japanese poetry form of three lines.
The first line is 5 syllables, the second line is 7 syllables, and the third line is 5 syllables.**

Haikus often focus on personal observations of nature.
Example:
Desert cactus blooms (5 syllables)
Colorful surprises peak (7 syllables)
To delight my eyes (5 syllables)

Now, let's have some fun! Write haikus about some of your own experiences.

In quiet I see (5)

A world under the surface (7)

_____ (5)

At the break of dawn (5)

The dogs are ready to go (7)

_____ (5)

Beauty lies within (5)

_____ (7)

_____ (5)

Coffee in the morn (5)

_____ (7)

_____ (5)

Now, write your own haikus

_____ (5)

_____ (7)

_____ (5)

_____ (5)

_____ (7)

_____ (5)

Writing a Haiku may be a perfect practice of daily mindfulness.

OPTIMAL WELL-BEING FOR SENIOR ADULTS II

Haiku Fun
Leader's Guide

PURPOSE
To challenge creative thinking skills by composing haikus.

POSSIBLE NAMES OF SESSIONS
- *How To Hai Ku*
- *Creative Thinking*
- *Haikus for You*

BACKGROUND INFORMATION
Creative expression can encourage a release of thoughts and feelings. Creative writing can unlock symbolic thinking. Writing within the safety of a group can provide a fun way to explore creativity.

ACTIVITY
1. Ask group members if they are familiar with the term "haiku."
2. Distribute handouts and pens or pencils.
3. Explain to group members that challenging one's creativity is excellent for stimulating the brain.
4. Proceed by working on the handout together as a group, fostering fun, creativity, and positive insights. Emphasize that haikus can be a mindfulness practice as they provide an avenue for making personal observations.
5. Share favorite haikus by posting them on a dry erase board, flyer, or bulletin board.

VARIATIONS
Divide group into thirds. Each participant will write the first line, and then will pass it to the second person to write the second line, who will then pass it to the third person to complete.

NOTES
_____
_____
_____
_____
_____
_____
_____
_____
_____
_____
_____
_____
_____
_____
_____

BONUS
Table of Contents and Corresponding Goals for Each Section

> "Age is a question of mind over matter.
> If you don't mind, it doesn't matter."
>
> ~ Leroy "Satchel" Paige

CERTIFICATE OF COMPLETION 131
To honor group participants.

My Mandala 133
To explore relaxation through coloring.

LEVEL OF UNDERSTANDING

Basic Level   Intermediate Level   High Level

OPTIMAL WELL-BEING FOR SENIOR ADULTS II

CERTIFICATE OF COMPLETION
Leader's Guide

PURPOSE
To acknowledge an individual's accomplishment.

POSSIBLE NAMES OF SESSIONS
- *Graduation Day*
- *A Proper Send Off!*
- *Gifts for You*

BACKGROUND INFORMATION
All people want and need to be recognized, even if they won't admit it! This certificate gives a tangible and memorable gift to those who have shown the dedication, perseverance, and commitment to complete a program.

ACTIVITY
1. Photocopy this certificate (preferably using a light color paper,) to recognize and acknowledge the group members who have completed the program.
2. Ask staff to sign notes in the blank spaces to wish them well.
3. Present the certificates, and give specific praise for a job well done.

VARIATIONS
Before awarding the certificates, ask each group member to give a "gift" to the graduates. It can be anything at all as long as it does not cost money and is heartfelt. *(Example: tranquility, travel to your heart's delight, be pain-free, sobriety, etc.)*

NOTES

My Mandala

Name_____

OPTIMAL WELL-BEING FOR SENIOR ADULTS II

My Mandala
Leader's Guide

PURPOSE
To explore the relaxation of coloring a mandala.

POSSIBLE NAMES OF SESSIONS
- *Relaxation*
- *Creative Expression*
- *Mandala Mindfulness*

BACKGROUND INFORMATION
Coloring can be relaxing, meditative, and enhance mindfulness by focusing on just the act of coloring. Learning how to gently redirect the mind to a single activity is a worthwhile and lifelong skill.

ACTIVITY
1. Photocopy this mandala and distribute it with gel pens, color pencils, and crayons, for individual and group relaxation.
2. Try playing soft music.
3. Explain to participants that coloring can be meditative in nature.
4. Suggest that completed mandalas can be a gift to self or to others, as well as a wall hanging.

VARIATIONS
Use completed mandalas for the front of a group member's notebook or folder or on the person's door or bulletin board, or laminate two together as a placemat.

NOTES
_____
_____
_____
_____
_____
_____
_____
_____
_____
_____
_____
_____
_____
_____
_____
_____
_____
_____

Whole Person Associates is the leading publisher of training resources for professionals who empower people to create and maintain healthy lifestyles. Our creative resources will help you work effectively with your clients in the areas of stress management, wellness promotion, mental health, and life skills.

Please visit us at our web site: **WholePerson.com**. You can check out our entire line of products, place an order, request our print catalog, and sign up for our monthly special notifications.

Whole Person Associates
800-247-6789
Books@WholePerson.com